REVISED & ENLARGED

FLY-TYING TIPS

EDITED BY DICK STEWART

ILLUSTRATIONS BY LARRY LARGAY

PUBLISHED BY MOUNTAIN POND PUBLISHING
NORTH CONWAY, NH
1993

Other books by Dick Stewart:
  Universal Fly Tying Guide
  Trolling Flies for Trout & Salmon (with Bob Leeman)
  The Hook Book
  Bass Flies
  Flies for Atlantic Salmon (with Farrow Allen)
  Flies for Steelhead (with Farrow Allen)
  Flies for Bass & Panfish (with Farrow Allen)
  Flies for Saltwater (with Farrow Allen)
  Flies for Trout (with Farrow Allen)

Mountain Pond Publishing
P.O. Box 797
North Conway, NH 03860
USA

Cover design by Larry Largay

Second Edition

ISBN 0-936644-19-2

TABLE OF CONTENTS

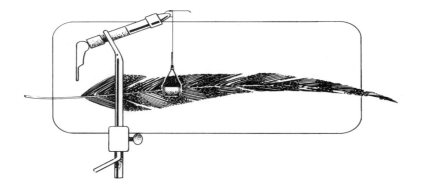

ACKNOWLEDGEMENTS

"Without being maudlin, I like to think that the fraternity of flytiers and fishermen is very special. A bond links us, one to the other, in all things relevant to our pursuits; and this bond should preclude the petty jealousy and envy that produce these "secrets" that others keep to themselves."

Eric Leiser
Fly-Tying Materials, 1973

This book is the product of a tremendous outpouring and sharing of ideas by fly tyers everywhere. As the former publisher of *American Angler* magazine I have been fortunate to have available a collection of the many fly-tying tips which appeared in the magazine over the past dozen years. These ideas constitute over half of this book's content. I am unable to credit the many individual tyers for their contributions (which in many cases ideas have been duplicated by various sources), but on behalf of the fly-tying community I would like to personally thank the hundreds of fellow fly tying enthusiasts who shared their ideas over the years.

This book represents only a portion of the many possible fly tying tips, for there are many good ideas which I've missed, many I've never learned, and there are many yet to be discovered. I hope this edition will be the continuation of an evolutionary process which will be updated from time to time as new ideas are received. Toward that end I will continue to encourage fly tyers everywhere to share their ideas.

Essential to the completion of this book were the contributions of the late Fran Stuart, an enthusiastic and fastidious fly tyer from Peterborough, New Hampshire. Fran provided significant editorial help, particularly through the use of reference material found in her extensive angling library. Shortly after her losing battle with cancer, Fran was named Angler of the Year by *Fly Rod & Reel* magazine.

Many of you will recognize the illustrations provided by Larry Largay of Thomaston, Maine. I am fortunate to work with an artist who is also an experienced fly tyer.

"I confess, no direction can be given to make a man of a dull capacity able to make a fly well . . . but to see a fly made by an artist in that kind, is the best teaching."

Izaak Walton
The Complete Angler, 1676 ed.

". . . . . no fly-fisherman can know the full extent of the pleasure of fly-fishing unless he does, or is at least able to, dress the flies he uses.

Fly-dressing has something else to recommend it. It acts in a truly remarkable way as a sedative at times of nervous disturbance and mental stress. There seems to be some influence generated in the touch of the feathers and silks, in the manipulations and in the concentration generally, which are associated with the making of flies, the effect of which is a soothing of jangled nerves, the allaying of care, the re-establishment of confidence and the revival of a sense of proportion. Thoughts may be as glum as the gloom of a December fog, as bitter as a January frost, or as stormy as the wind and rain of a bleak February day; but if there is to be had, in the quiet privacy of a room, a table, with all the requisites of fly-making ready to hand, with a good light by which to see and a comfortable seat on which to sit, there are the means available to recover tranquillity and contentment. This is not a fanciful picture. It is an indubitable fact."

Dr. Thomas Edwin Pryce-Tannatt
Meditations (in an Arm-Chair) of a Middle-aged Angler, 1932

"Fly tying is both an art form and a science: an art form of necessity and a science by evolution. Perhaps its best quality is filling that awful limbo of the sportsman's fifth season—the time falling between the last of deer season and the first of trout season—for it is then that the fly rods, impatient to go, fairly twist in their cases, and the fly chest buzzes with dozens of flies still untried from last season."

J. Edson Leonard
The Essential Fly Tier, 1976

THE TYING ENVIRONMENT

"FLY TYING. The technique of fastening various materials on a hook to suggest real or fancied flies, or other insects or food objects for the purpose of deceiving fish."

A. McClane
The Wise Fishermen's Encyclopedia, 1951

LESSENING EYE STRAIN

Even if you don't spend long hours at your tying bench, a non-glare, neutral background is essential to reducing eye-strain. The vinyl protective covering that draftsmen use on their drawing boards is ideal for the top of your tying table. Available at most art and drafting supply stores, it comes in several sizes, and is green on one side and cream colored on the other. Use it green side up when tying light colored flies, and cream side up when tying dark patterns. It cleans up easily with soap and warm water, and less head cement on the dining room table will be appreciated by everyone in the family.

TRAP-DOOR TYING TABLE

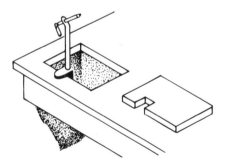

The placement of a hole or "trap door" in the middle of a tying bench is a great convenience. A 6" x 8" hole 6 inches from the front edge of the table allows for comfortable tying as well as providing a chute for waste materials trimmed from the fly. In order to hold the plastic bag that serves as wastebasket, place four screws, with heads exposed, on

the underside, and a rubber band will hold the plastic bag in place. If you want to convert the table back to a solid top, the piece that was originally cut out can be replaced if you install a couple of cleats underneath to support it. An added benefit of having the vise mounted away from the front edge of the table is that tools and tying materials seem to fall to the floor less often!

NEAT IS NICER

It takes only a few minutes to make a world-class mess of a fly-tying area. The head cement bottle is tipped over. A box of hooks is spilled. Scissors are lost somewhere in the clutter. The stiletto is covered with hardened varnish when it is needed to remove a couple of errant barbules from the eye of a tiny dry fly. By training (or forcing) yourself to be deliberate, precise and neat at the tying table most disasters can be avoided. Cap the varnish bottle after each use. Close the box of hooks after removing the quantity that is immediately needed. Before it hardens, clean the varnish off the stiletto. Hang up the scissors if they are not being held in your hand. The difference may be one less fly tied during a session, but you'll soon appreciate having everything in its place and ready for use.

GIMME SOME LIGHT

Use an etcher's screen for diffused lighting. Such a screen is simple to construct and consists of a frame on which is stretched a piece of pale blue glazed linen. It is not difficult to dye linen a pale blue color if only white linen is available in a particular region of the country. (The etcher's screen is often used in architect's offices). Just support the frame between the source of light and the work. This procedure, using tungsten light, provides for an excellent source of soft and non-eye-straining illumination.

SIGHT SAVER

Few fly tyers have a proper set-up for lighting and background. Use a piece of wood with a 1/8" wide saw kerf about 1/2" deep to hold a piece of tempered hardboard cut to 8" x 10". Either paint the board or glue colored poster stock to it in colors that make the fly easier to see. Use a light background for dark and vice versa for light flies. Pale green is an excellent all around color. Your eyes will focus on the fly instead of the distracting materials lying on your bench. As a note, if you sidelight or backlight your fly you will see more detail with ease.

HANDY MAGNETIC STRIP

By affixing a strip of magnetic tape near your fly-tying area you will have a handy place to temporarily hold either your current selection of hooks, or else those stray hooks which invariably appear out of nowhere. It's also a handy spot for work-in-process or for storing flies as head cement dries.

USE LITTER BAGS

Here's an easy way to keep your bench and work area free of debris. Obtain a plastic litter bag—the type with a hole in the top so as to attach to an interior car door handle. These 8 1/2" x 11" bags are often given away by fish and game departments, and concerned advertisers, to control litter. Slide the bag down over your vise. It'll hang below the

tying area, as you trim excess materials from flies, the trimmings will drop into the bag.

REVERSE IMAGE

A mirror, either hand-held, or better yet, one mounted on a flexible arm, can be a tremendous aid to the fly tyer. On complex or difficult patterns such as traditional Atlantic salmon flies or streamers the mirror allows a close inspection of the side of your fly not normally seen. Using a mirror helps you find mistakes during the tying process so that they may be corrected before it's too late.

SHAVING MIRROR

A very useful accessory when tying flies is a make-up or shaving mirror.

This mirror is 5" in diameter, comes with a metal stand, is double sided, costs only a few dollars, and is found in most discount stores. One side is a regular mirror and the other side enlarges the image.

Placed on your tying bench behind your vise and out of the way, it allows you to see the opposite side of your fly without rotating or turning the vise around.

HANDLING WASTE

If you tie at a regular desk here's an idea which might help you keep organized. Instead of a trash bag or waste basket, use the center drawer of your tying desk. Simply open it as much or as little as needed. When clipping deer hair just open it and clip away. Just by closing the drawer you have a neat room.

STACKING WITHOUT SCARS

When using a hair stacker it's all to easy to mar the tabletop on which you're tapping the stacker. An easy solution is to cover the bottom of the stacker with felt. First score the bottom of the stacker with emery paper to provide a good gripping surface, then a light coat of Elmer's White or similar adhesive, and press the bottom of the stacker firmly onto the piece of felt. Let dry overnight and trim neatly. I have just discovered some self-stick felt at the hardware store which will also do the trick.

DOING IT RIGHT

Fly tying has been a favorite activity for more than 18 years. When I started, any assistance, aside from what could be learned from the few available books was almost non-existent, as were quality tools and materials. From time to time a friend and I would get together for an evening's tying and to exchange techniques and tips—helpful but limited. Recently I signed up for an intermediate level fly tying course, taught by a well-known instructor. I spent two tiring, challenging, informative and fun-filled days with ten other fly tyers of varying skill and experience and came away a far better tyer than before. Treat yourself! Spend the time and learn how to overcome some of the plaguing problems which keep your flies in the "sunfish league."

CLEAN HANDS

This tip is one that we all take for granted, but it is important. Always wash your hands with soap and water before you sit down to tie. The naturally occurring oils in human skin will discolor floss and thread, and often this discoloration does not become apparent until the fly is finished.

MAGNIFIERS

Even if you don't tie really small flies, an inexpensive pair of magnifying glasses are handy. They are available at many sporting goods stores, listed in many catalogs, and sometimes can be purchased at your local drug store. You'll be amazed at how much easier it is to pick out trapped hackle fibres, trim errant dubbing, and check your flies for stray threads when a size 16 fly is magnified by a factor of two.

BARGAIN TABLE

While searching for a desk to use as my fly-tying headquarters, I happened on a sewing-machine table, minus the machine, at a yard sale. I bought it for the grand sum of $12, and it has worked better than I had hoped. The well in the center that once held the machine now holds a plastic bag, taped securely at the edges, to catch all the clippings and cut off bits; the drawers hold tools, hooks and the like, and the unfolded top gives me a good big work surface, to hold spools, bottles, and materials.

BIODEGRADABLE DRYING RACK

Not only biodegradable but low-cost, light weight and portable. The ubiquitous Post-It note, (3-M Corporation), available at any office supply store coast to coast, will stick to the edge of the tying bench or table. The points of finished flies can be stuck through the opposite edge of the Post-It and left to dry undisturbed. Each piece will hold a half-dozen salmon flies, or up to a dozen small dries.

DON'T LOSE THAT FLY

Do you ever lose newly tied flies in the clutter of feathers and fur? Or, have you had to search the floor looking for a dropped fly? Cut a length of mono-filament or tippet material about six inches long. (The diameter is dependent on the size of the eye on the hooks you're using.) With a match or lighter, heat one end of the mono until it forms a bead. When the fly is finished but still in the vise, insert the unbeaded end of the mono through the eye of the fly. (This insures not only that you won't drop the fly, but also that there's no varnish clogging the eye.) Multiple flies can be put on the same piece of mono, and by inserting the mono (with flies) into a clip type clothespin they can be hung to dry.

EYE-LEVEL TOOL RACK

Try putting a few small magnets on the shade of your tying lamp, and using them to hold your bodkin, your scissors, or other tying tools when you're not using them. That way the tools stay out of the clutter and are easy to find. Another use for these magnets is to hold finished flies while the heads are drying. Magnets can be found on the bottom of old shower curtain liners.

CATCHER'S MITT FOR THE LAP

If you're tired of dropping tools and hooks, and even more tired of sweeping up the mess under your bench, try using a shop apron. Attach the lower edge of the apron to the edge of your table, and when you seat yourself at the bench, put on the neck loop. Just make sure that the apron is long enough to form a sort of trough in your lap to catch everything! When you finish tying, dump the pieces of feather, floss, tinsel, hair, etc. into the waste basket. No more tracking scrap throughout the house.

HANDSOME HEAD CEMENT HOLDER

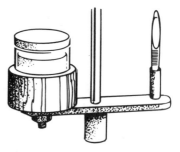

A container of head cement that is always being moved around on the bench is an invitation to disaster, and besides, the threads of the jar are usually gummed up. By constructing the holder as shown in the drawing, the cement is untippable and out of the way, but very accessible when needed. I use a fairly wide-mouthed jar because I can better see the surface of the liquid when I am reaching for a small drop of cement. I have placed the jar in a recess bored to the jar's diameter, in a wooden disk which in turn is bolted and glued to a "boom" which has a 3/4" dowel cemented into a recess on the bottom. This dowel is drilled to the diameter of the vise shaft (usually 3/8") and the entire assembly rotates around the shaft. On the side opposite the jar holder I have attached a tube to hold my tweezers, but you may opt for a holder for your scissors, a bobbin, or whatever. The entire assembly swings out of the way when not needed, it can't spill, and there is no glue on the lid or on the threads; after two months of use I can still open the jar with one hand.

CURING ODORIFEROUS EMANATIONS

If you got some strong-smelling "Soap on a Rope" from your favorite aunt at Christmas, try putting it in your tying area. It sure smells better than mothballs, and I'll bet your family members will approve.

SMOOTHING FINGERS

There is nothing more aggravating than fraying a piece of floss or thread due to an unnoticed spot of rough skin on your fingers. This annoyance is especially prevalent during the winter months. I keep an emery board at the side of my tying table to use before I start to handle flosses or thread. A couple of rubs on the emery board and my fingers are smooth enough not to fray even the most delicate flosses.

FOAM CORE STORAGE

Foam Core, which is sheet plastic foam with heavy paper laminated to either side, makes a dandy organizer for all your tying tools. It's inexpensive stuff, available at builders' supply stores, picture framing shops, etc., and can be cut any size and shape your heart desires. Tools stuck into it are easier to find than ones lying down on the tying table where they take on chameleon-like qualities. If you want a thicker piece, just cut two (or three) pieces and Pliobond them together. When the surface gets too chewed up, just Pliobond another piece on top.

A CURE FOR WINTER FINGERS?

I doubt that there's a tyer in the north temperate zone who does not suffer from dry, chapped, rough skin on his or her hands and fingers during the winter months. Floss, threads, dubbing and tempers fray as tying becomes more and more difficult and the results less satisfactory. Well, at my local stationery store, of all places, I found a product called "Gatherette," a fingertip moistener for bank tellers and cashiers that is sensational for the fly tyer. It contains glycerine, glycol and lanolin among other things, and it makes handling our fragile materials a cinch, regardless of the season. Most highly recommended.

SPEED AND UNIFORMITY

These are two things that all tyers should develop. A great aid toward this goal is to put a piece of white cardboard on your tying table and mark the surface to indicate the correct lengths for floss, tinsel, and wings for a variety of hook sizes. This way, when you sit down to tie #6 Gray Ghosts for example, the correct material lengths are at your fingertips. An additional benefit is that you waste less material.

PREVENTING BLOWAWAYS

When tying outdoors, for demonstrations, seminars, or just because you want to, one little puff of wind will blow your materials into the next county. To avoid this, attach spring type clothespins to everything that is

13

not naturally weighted. The clothespin acts like an anchor and holds the weightless stuff - feathers, packets of dubbing, small pieces of fur, etc. - firmly where you want them.

TYING DESK
As my family grew and left home, space became available for a permanent fly-tying area, and the question arose, "what should I use for a bench?" A computer desk fills the bill perfectly. For about $75 I got a large, flat work surface and plenty of storage, too.

GROCERY BAG WASTE CONTAINER

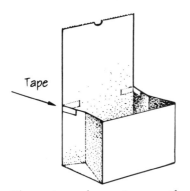

Tape

The universal, omnipresent brown paper grocery bag makes a great waste container in front of your vise. After cutting it as per the drawing, I add Scotch tape reinforcements at the corners. Use one until it's full, throw it away, and make another!

SMOOTH FINGERS
Here's a final step to be used after using a pumice stone or emery board to smooth away the rough skin on your fingers before starting to tie. Any drug store will have a product called "New Skin". I put a little of this on my fingers. It's an antiseptic liquid with the consistency of Dave's Flexament. It dries smooth, clear and flexible so it bends with your fingers and will even fill in deep cracks in chapped fingers. It can

even be used as a substitute for head cement.

BACK SAVER
An afternoon or evening spent at the tying bench can often result in a sore back. An ergonomically designed chair, commonly called a Norwegian Posture Chair, may provide relief. These odd-looking chairs are available from most office furniture outlets, and are a huge help to those of us who have bad backs.

RECYCLING TIP
When a box of facial tissues, Kleenex, or the like, is empty, I tape the box on the front of my tying table for a waste container. The slot in the top keeps the odd bits of feathers and furs from blowing around, and when the box is filled, it's trashed and another empty one is put into service.

LAP DESK

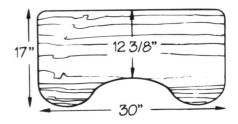

17"   12 3/8"

30"

Here's a pattern for a tying board that can be used in your favorite easy chair. It is cut in a kidney shape; the curve allows the board to be pulled close to your body. Make it about 30 inches long—big enough to fit securely over the arms of your chair. You can tailor make your board in any size you want. Use 3/8-inch plywood, sand it well, and paint it. It can also be covered with formica, leather, or it can be stained. If you use a screw-on vise, Formica prevents the wood from getting chewed up.

STORAGE & ORGANIZATION

"In addition to (other) advantages (of fly tying), that of cleanliness must not be omitted. How greatly preferable is the simple formation of an artificial fly of feathers and fur, to the unpleasantness attendant upon baiting a hook with worm, maggot, or paste."

George Cole Bainbridge
The Fly Fisher's Guide, 4th ed., 1860

COASTERS HOLD MORE THAN GLASSES

An effective method of removing very small flies from the tying vise without crushing the hackle or messing up the head cement is by using a cardboard beer coaster. When you've finished lacquering the head of the fly, push the point of the hook into the edge of the coaster, open the vise, and place coaster and fly on a flat surface to dry. The edges of a coaster can hold between 20 and 40 flies, depending on their size. By not handling these tiny, freshly tied and lacquered flies and allowing the cement to harden, a nicer looking product results.

FOAM TYING STAND

Many tyers keep a chunk of styrofoam on their benches. It is cheap, easily obtainable and serves a multitude of uses, from holding tools to holding finished flies. A far better type of foam is something called Plastazote, available from BIOQUIP, 1320 East Franklin Avenue, El Segundo, CA 90245. Item 1028P is a 3/8" by 16" by 18" sheet that costs less than ten dollars. To keep the Plastazote from migrating around your bench top, cement a piece of it to a one

by six. Then, if you cement the loop side of some Velcro to the Plastazote and the hook side to the bottom of your bottle of head cement, you'll solve the problem of spilled cement, too.

BIOT MINDER

A neat and decorative way of having goose biots at hand is to make Christmas trees! Using small dowels or skewers, wire the small end of the biot strip to the top of the stick. Spiral the strip down the dowel, and secure it with another piece of wire (or string). The resulting mini tree displays the entire strip so that cutting off just the sizes you require is simple. And a jar of these "trees," in various colors, makes an interesting and amusing bit of decoration on the tying table.

ELIMINATE GREASY MATERIALS

Most often when you purchase necks or skins from a fly tying supply house the materials have been processed to substantially remove any excess fats or grease. At times you might acquire some materials which are still a bit greasy and unpleasant to work with. You can address this problem by taking the following steps:

1. Check for any noticeable residues of fat on the skin and, if present, scrape them away with a knife.

2. Thoroughly wash the material in warm, soapy water, rinse and press the material between paper towels to remove most moisture.

3. Place the material, hair or feather side down, on a paper towel. Take some borax, or regular table salt, and spread it onto the skin side of your material, lightly rubbing it into the skin. This draws out excess oils.

4. Once dry, brush away the salt (or borax) and you will have much cleaner materials to work with.

HOOK STORAGE RACK

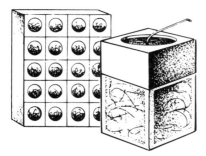

Any office supply store stocks the square plastic containers with magnetic tops used to dispense one paper clip at a time. They will perform the same function for hooks. You can build a wooden grid to hold the dispensers on their sides. Arrange the hooks by size in columns down and by shank length in rows across. Each container holds a hundred or more hooks and allows easy access without worry of spilling.

BAG-A-FLY

Try putting all the materials for one pattern in a Ziploc bag. If you have limited time to tie, it's very quick to pull out the bag with the materials for, let's say, the Black Ghost, rather than opening umpteen boxes and drawers hunting up the yellow hackle for the tail and throat, the flat tinsel for the rib, the white streamer hackle for the wing, etc. And if you travel for a living, you'll be able to produce a lot of flies without bringing large quantities of materials with you. Saves time, saves space.

HOOK STORAGE

As a way to save space in your portable fly tying kit, try using seven day pill reminder boxes to store hooks. The smaller ones are 1/2" deep, 7/8" wide, and 4 1/2" long. Each compartment has its own lid and holds hooks one model of hook from size 10 through size 22. Purchase a box for each type of hook you anticipate might be needed.

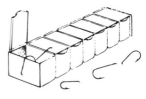

HOT . . .

To avoid any insect infestation of your valuable fly-tying materials, put newly purchased fur or feathers into a microwave oven for a minute at low or medium setting. There is absolutely no damage to your materials and any lurking moth or beetle larvae just waiting to destroy your precious supply of materials is "nuked" into oblivion. Of course, you still have to store the sanitized stuff carefully—use either glass jars or plastic bags. This tip is especially valuable if you are a collector of road kills!

AND COLD

Are your tying materials infested with bugs? Do you dare use dangerous pesticides on your precious materials? A much better way to alleviate this buggy problem is to freeze your materials. Once you discover your materials are contaminated, simply place all the infected materials in a plastic bag and place it in the freezer for a couple of days. This will kill all the bugs without leaving any foul odors or dangerous chemicals on your materials. Be sure to let your materials completely thaw before attempting to tie with them.

MUFFIN-PAN MATERIALS HOLDER

Nothing is more frustrating than not being able to locate all of the materials you've selected to tie a particular fly. One suggestion that also speeds up your tying is to select and sort your materials into a muffin, or cupcake pan. You can even sort using each row for a different size fly.

TACK BOX FOR STORAGE

Mail order kennel supply houses as well as some Agway stores carry wood or aluminum chests that are intended for use by dog handlers to carry their extra leashes, combs, brushes, shampoos, blowers etc. to dog shows. Available in several sizes and interior configurations, they make absolutely wonderful chests for all your tying tools and materials. An added benefit is that the aluminum ones, besides being very strong, are very light, so that you're able to carry a tremendous amount of stuff, including heavy pedestal bases, illuminated magnifiers, etc., and not break your back picking it up.

STORING MATERIALS FOR TRAVELLING

You'll need a 3-ring loose leaf binder, preferably with 3 inch rings, some one gallon Ziploc bags, a hole punch and 1 1/2 inch duct tape. Apply a strip of duct tape along one side of each bag and punch 3 holes in it to correspond to the spacing of the notebook rings. In order to eliminate "ballooning" of the bags when closing them, make a very small cut in the edge of each bag. Use a Dymo Labelmaker to label each bag's contents, placing the label close to the edge of the bag. When going on vacation or to fly tying seminars, this is a convenient method for orderly storage.

ANOTHER USE FOR THE PILL-BOX

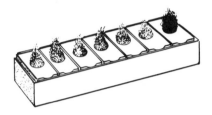

Purchase a seven-day plastic pill box at a local pharmacy and using a sharp 1/4" drill, bore a hole in the top flap of each compartment. This should be done by hand rather than with an electric drill so as not to crack or tear the plastic flaps. After filling the individual compartments with dubbing, use a pair of tweezers to pull it up through the small hole to get it started. Then, each time you take a pinch of dubbing, more will automatically pull itself up through the hole. Mark the front of each compartment with the color or blend.

If you happen to have a magnetic strip attached to your tying bench, you can glue another one on the bottom of your new dubbing dispenser and hold it in place, although it's still easy to remove when it's time to refill. This system certainly beats sorting through bags of dubbing.

ZIPLOC STORAGE

Do you open your box marked wool or chenille only to find a tangled mess? If so consider obtaining some Ziploc sandwich or storage bags and sorting your materials into these. Leave one short end protruding from the almost-closed zip opening and you'll have instant access to your conveniently stored supply.

FILM CONTAINERS

Put your old film containers to good use by making a hole of approximately 1/4" diameter in the top and use them as moth ball holders for your material storage boxes. This method keeps the moth ball odor to a minimum and keeps the moth balls out of direct contact with your materials while providing adequate discouragement for any would-be residents in your valuable feathers and furs.

It's a simple idea but it works well and keeps the mothball odor in your tying room tolerable.

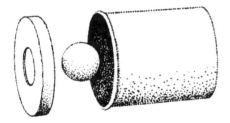

GRASPING AT STRAWS

Most tyers store their dubbing in poly bags. Convenient, but in time, the bags seem to scatter, so that searching for the needed shade becomes something of a treasure hunt. Try repackaging the dubbing in plastic soda straws! A plastic straw, cut to a 4" length, will contain an entire 3" x 4" bag of dubbing. The material is pushed tightly into the straw, using the end of a bodkin, crochet hook or small rod. Force the dubbing to the end of the straw (keep it from escaping with your index finger). Keep pushing in the dubbing until the straw is full, and then mark the name of the material on the outside of the straw

with a felt tipped pen. To retrieve the dubbing, simply twist the straw between your thumb and index finger to force a bit out the end of the straw and pinch off the amount needed. Eight of these dubbing straws will fit easily into an empty 3" x 4" poly bag.

FLOSS HOLDER

Your nearest sewing supplies or crafts store should have a gadget called "Easy-Bob" (Triad Corp., Box 188, Alda, NE 68810), and perhaps other brand names as well, which will cost you in the vicinity of two and a half bucks. You can spend lots more for gadgets that prove to be only occasionally useful, but this one is just about indispensable. It keeps any material that comes in lengths clean, neat and readily available. Use one stack for your yarns, one for flosses, another for wires and leads.

ANOTHER CLEANUP TIP

Candice Bergen, as the TV character Murphy Brown, recently exclaimed that she had so much trash in her yard that it "looked like a goat exploded." If this also describes your tying area, here's a possible way out of the mess. Buy a selection of pegboard hooks and a piece of pegboard large enough to fit the available wall space. Install the board and sort your materials into plastic bags. Then hang the bags on the hooks. This makes for a very flexible storage system, so that if you know you'll be tying streamers for the next few evenings, you can hang those materials close to hand, and when you're ready to tie dries, you can rehang those materials nearby. You'll be able to see at a glance if you have on hand the materials needed for your next pattern, and once you get your bench cleaned up, (it's not a lot of fun, but it is necessary) you'll find that it really helps to see what you have.

However, when your pegboard has more materials on it than your fly shop, it's time to think up an alternative storage scheme.

FILM CONTAINERS AGAIN

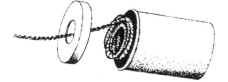

One more use for the plastic container which is supplied with 35mm roll film. Do you ever find that hooks, or bits of feather and fur, become entangled in your various yarns? It seems that a skein of yarn attracts unwanted clippings; or hooks become hopelessly entwined. You can eliminate this by cutting a small hole in the top of an old film container—a hole the approximate diameter of the yarn you wish to use. By stuffing the container full of yarn, and allowing only the top inch to extend out the hole, the quantity inside remains clean, yet easily available.

CANDY BOX STORAGE

Found near the checkout counters in most supermarkets are various brands of mint candies, sold in nifty small plastic boxes. After you've eaten the mints, the boxes make great storage containers for hooks and other small items. The labels peel off easily, the lids latch firmly, they can easily be labelled with their contents, and best of all, they stack or can be stored in a larger container.

STORAGE BOXES

No one ever seems to have enough boxes in which to store materials. Collections of fur and feathers seem to grow faster than our ability to find containers in which to put them. In the "Closet Shop" of most chain stores you can buy clear plastic shoe and sweater storage boxes. For a couple of dollars each these make excellent materials storage containers. They stack one on top of the other, are easy to label, look neat, and best of all, protect your stuff against the assaults of bugs and dust. Don't forget to put moth balls in each box before storing your materials.

SPOOLED MATERIALS

You can use old typewriter ribbon spools to keep many types of wools, yarns, etc., in order. These spools hold several yards of material and take up very little space.

To store the spools push rods through the holes in the centers of the spools and keep them in horizontal or vertical stacks on your desk.

NO-SLIP DRYING RACK

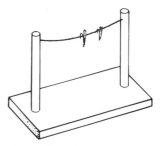

Use ordinary bead chain, two wooden dowels, and a piece of 1" x 4" wood, and construct a drying rack like that in the drawing. You can hang a lot of flies of various weights and lengths, and even if the chain sags slightly, the beads will keep your finished flies from sliding together.

WASTE-BAG HOLDER

Here is a simple but useful tip used to keep a tying bench clean. Adapt an embroidery hoop to become a waste holder by attaching a plastic bag and then securing the completed unit to a desk drawer. Considering that this device results of a cleaner work area, you might even have the embroidery hoop donated by a family member.

FLASHY STORAGE

Flashabou, Crystal Flash and other "flashy" materials are a pain to store in such a manner that they stay straight, don't get crumpled, and are available for use. The 7-11 stores sell a drink called a "Slurpee" which comes with a special drinking straw that is flared at one end. Slit the straw lengthwise with a razor blade. Most of the flashy materials come bound with a plastic clip at one end. Insert this clip into the flared end of the straw and pull forward until all the material is encased in the straw.

This method is cheap and space-conserving, and identification of the material is easy.

BENCHTOP ANCHOR
Florist's clay is a godsend for anchoring tippables on your bench. A small dab of this clay on the bottom of the head cement bottle will prevent a major disaster, and another hunk of it is equally handy for stabbing your bodkin into between uses.

NO MORE TANGLES

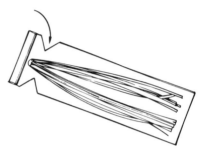

To prevent Krystal Flash or Flashabou from becoming a tangled mess when being used, simply leave the material in the poly bag it comes in and cut a notch in each upper corner. When tying with these materials, use a dubbing needle to pull as many strands as you need and clip them off at the notch in the bag.

ORGANIZING SPOOLS
A "gravity feed nail polish rack," as found at cosmetic counters, has several rows of slots that are slightly larger than the spools of material we fly tyers use. Often these racks are trashed when the polish is sold out, and they really do work well. Check at your local drug or chain store.

OATMEAL CONTAINERS
Quaker oatmeal, besides being good for keeping your cholesterol down, is sold in nifty plastic-coated cylinders. The container has a nice, durable white

plastic snap-on lid which is easy to write on with any permanent marker. These containers look great, store conveniently, and cost nothing if you eat oatmeal like your mother told you to.

ANCHORED WAX

If you use dubbing wax, then this is a great way to keep the tube handy but out of the way. Tape the cap to the stem of your vise. When you need the wax all you need do is pull the container out of its lid, use it, and replace the container in the lid when you're finished. It's always handy but never in the way or buried in the clutter.

STREAMER RACK

Where to hang your finished streamers while waiting for the head cement to dry? If you or anyone you know works in an office where adding machines are used, you can have all the "streamer stands" you'll ever need. Most paper tape for these machines comes on a segmented plastic core, and there just happens to be 12 equally spaced seg-

ments in each core. These are long enough to hold even 6X long streamers, and will keep each wet-headed fly blemish-free until dry and ready to store. If you are into production tying, a number of these rollers will help you keep track of the number of dozen flies you have tied so far, and they're free for the asking.

WASH YOUR NECKS

Try washing your necks and saddles in a light solution of Woolite. This not only removes any dirt and grime from the feathers but the individual feathers will palmer and wind around the hook much better when they are soft and clean. After rinsing well, dry them, first by blowing the feathers lightly with a hair drier and then laying them on a sweater drying rack. These gadgets are netting and tubing affairs available at any chain store. They make ideal drying racks as the netting allows air to circulate around all sides of the necks and saddles.

TINSEL & FLOSS DISPENSER

The small spools that some brands of floss and tinsels come on are a real nuisance to handle - there's no place to affix the loose end of the material and often it unwinds and gets mangled and unusable. The solution for me was to use 35 mm film cassettes - not the neat little plastic containers with snap-on caps but the metal containers that hold the film. The spools are a nice snug fit and the material dispenses easily through the film slot.

ZIP-LOC DUBBING DISPENSER

Your local hardware store will be happy to sell you an eyelet tool for a few bucks. Bring it home and then, with a supply of small Zip Loc bags on hand, install an eyelet through one side of a bag, smooth side of the eyelet facing in. Fill with dubbing of your choice. When wanted, the dubbing will feed out through the eyelet in just the amount you need - no waste. For travelling, you can fit many different small bags into a large one and never lack for just the shade of dubbing you want.

PENCIL FLY HOLDERS

By pressing the eraser end of a lead pencil onto the point of a fly you can neatly remove it from the vise without crushing hackles or messing up wet lacquer. This is particularly important when creating epoxy bodies. Once the point of the hook is embedded in the eraser, the pencil can be laid over the edge of your tying table or placed in a cup. A dozen pencils will hold a dozen flies, to dry and harden with no chance of marring the finish.

FILING TYING MATERIALS

Many tiers use Zip-Lock bags to separate materials. By inserting into each bag a piece of light cardboard with the name of the contents printed clearly across the top, you'll have a ready-made filing system. By standing the bags into a box that is low enough to make the "labels" easily readable, and high enough to hold all the bags in place, your tying table is a lot neater, there is less waste and best of all, materials don't get buried on the table top.

FULLERS EARTH

This stuff is great if any of your tying fur is producing rancid oil due to incomplete curing of the hide. It can be purchased at hardware stores and pharmacies, and a layer of the stuff applied to the non-hair side of the hide will absorb the offending oil.

SPOOL STORAGE

A sewing supply catalog was the source for a vertical thread storage rack. It holds about 50 spools of thread, floss and the like, and best of all, takes up very little space.

BURL-Y TOOL RACK

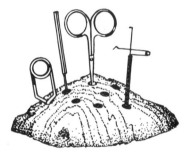

Trying to find a specific tool which has buried iteself beneath the pile of materials on your tying desk is a pain. Cut a burl knob off a tree root, clean it up, drill holes in it to hold all your tying tools. You will find that an evening's tying now goes a lot more smoothly. The burl is not only good looking, but plenty heavy enough to keep from toppling over when all the tools are in place.

TOOLS
MADE & MAKESHIFT

"It is open (to) question whether a vise ought to be used in tying . . . but the simplest answer is that, even if one habitually dresses flies with the aid of a vise, one should, on occasion, be able to dispense with it, so that, given a hook, wax, some silk and a few feathers, one is completely independent of light, place and heavy luggage."

Eric Taverner
Salmon Fishing, 1931

FLY SCRUBBER

Want to give your flies that "buggy" look? Tired of pulling out the fluff with a needle? Try the Fly Scrubber.

Materials needed are a popsicle stick, glue, and the hook side of a 1/2" wide Velcro strip. Glue the Velcro onto one half of one side of the popsicle stick. When the glue is dry trim the Velcro flush with the stick edges. Use the Fly Scrubber to tease out dubbing fibers—just draw the Velcro across the fly for a "buggy" result.

DISPOSABLE BRUSH

Something called a "chenille stem," sold at crafts stores makes a great disposable brush - for epoxy, Flexament, paint - anything for which you'd use a regular brush. It may look like a pipe cleaner but the fibers are not cotton, so there's a lot less shedding. Stroke the last inch or so of the stem before using so as to remove any stray fibers, use it in place of a brush, and when finished, cut off the inch or so that you've used, stroke the new end to dislodge any loose fibers, and you have a new applicator.

DUBBING TEASER

Take a wire rifle bore cleaner—the one with a short wire spiral around the bore—and stick this into a wine bottle cork be used for the handle.

Use this tool to pick out fur bodies. Works great for fuzzy nymphs.

ANTLER BODKIN

Bodkins made of a needle and section of deer antler will not roll and are easy to pick up. The business end of the bodkin is a sewing needle.

Drill a 1/16" hole at least 1/2" deep into the antler. Dip the eye of the needle into epoxy glue and insert in the hole with a twisting motion to work the glue down into the hole.

Needles come in various sizes; bodkins with large needles are used for large bass bugs and very fine-needled bodkins for applying head cement to small flies.

To make a cleaner to remove dried head cement from the bodkins, stuff a small container with 4/0 steel wool. To clean the bodkin, poke it into the steel wool until it's clean. Make sure the container is longer than the needle. If the needle hits the bottom of the container it could damage the tip.

FUR-BLENDING BRUSHES

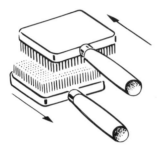

Small electric blenders are great for making dubbing mixes of fine and medium textured fur and synthetics, but if the material is too long or too coarse, the blender clogs. Try using two wire brushes that customarily are used for brushing dogs! These readily available tools have fine wire teeth, angled at the tip into the shape of a poorly formed "7." Put the material to be blended on the teeth of the first brush, and using the second one wire teeth down, pull the brushes across each other, drawing the material between the teeth. After several passes, the dubbing is completely blended. This same technique is used in carding wool, preparatory to spinning it.

HAIR COMPRESSOR

Here is a hair compressing tool which has been particularly useful for working on smaller flies. You may find this tool solves your problems, is easy to make and easier to use.

Take a pair of tweezers (the larger the better) and cut off the ends bearing serrations. After carefully smoothing them, bend about 1/4 inch of each end 90 degrees toward the other. With a triangular file put a small notch in each end, then fully smooth those notches.

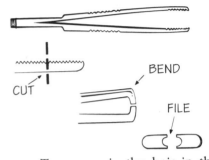

To use, spin the hair in the accustomed manner. Squeeze the notches onto the hook shank and push. This one tool can be used on any size hook but works best on smaller hooks (Irresistibles and Muddlers, as opposed to bass bugs) unless you pad the end which fits into your palm.

MONO THREADER

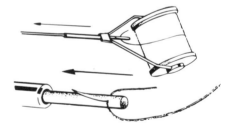

In years past most fly tying threads were not prewaxed and a bobbin could be threaded by a strong sucking breath on the end of the barrel. But today a residue of wax often builds up in the bobbin barrel, necessitating the use of some type of bobbin threader.

A makeshift threader can be fabricated with a length of heavy monofilament and a sharp razor blade. An shallow angular slit is cut into the monofilament a short ways from the end. The mono is fed through the barrel of the bobbin, the thread hooked into the slit, and then the mono/threader pulls the thread out of the barrel. The bobbin is loaded with tying thread and ready for action.

TWO-WAY TOOL

For those who use whip finishers to tie off the heads of flies, there is a way to turn it into two tools in one, saving the step of having to go to your scissors or blade to cut the thread.

At the butt end of most whip finishers there is a metal tab that acts as a "nut and washer" holding the spinning collar onto the metal spine of the tool. Take a small triangular shaped rattail file and put a notch into the tab by running the file over both sides of the very end. This creates a sharp notch which can be used by simply slipping it onto the taut thread and pushing back towards the bend of the hook. The tautness is important because when the thread is severed, the loose end slips back under the wraps of the whip finish leaving a neat looking head.

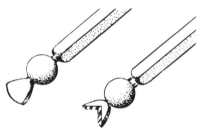

DUBBING-NEEDLE CLEANER

Is your dubbing needle often covered with dried head cement. Here's a solution. Take a stainless steel pot scrubber (Amway's Scrub Buds works well, and doesn't dull your needle) and stuff as much of it as you can into a 35 mm film cannister. Cut off the excess with tin snips. If you've used the old metal style cannister, pierce the lid with your dubbing needle; if you've used the plastic cannister, punch a hole in the top with a hole punch. Replace the lid on the filled cannister and you're done.

After using the needle to apply head cement, shove it into the cannister. When next you need it, the needle will be clean and smooth. Build a holder on your tying table to anchor the head cement and needle cleaner side-by-side, then you can use them with one hand

HIGH-VISIBILITY BOBBIN THREADER

Often, your bobbin threader may consist of nothing more than a doubled-over piece of piano wire. Nothing wrong with that except it is difficult to keep track of amid all the other metal tools on the tying table. The dilemma is solved by embedding the folded ends of the wire into a cork. The cork is then painted fluorescent orange, and is easily found amid the clutter.

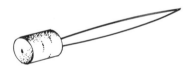

PORCUPINE BODKIN

A great bodkin for applying head cement is made from a large porcupine quill. They are very light and the end gradually tapers to an extremely fine point. It is this very fine taper that allows the application of tiny amounts of cement. It is especially effective with a cement such as Dave's Flexament, which is often difficult to apply in minute amounts on very small flies. The cement is also much easier to scrape off a quill point than a steel bodkin, leaving a clean point for the next application.

RUBBER-BAND HACKLE GUARD

Here is a simple, yet effective, hackle guard made of the simplest of materials. The materials needed are plastic drinking straws of various sizes, assorted rubber bands, and a 6" length of stiff wire.

Form a small hook on one end of the wire. Cut the straw into 1 inch pieces. Insert the wire through the straw and hook onto a rubber band. Pull the rubber band through the straw leaving large loops on each end. The illustrations show how to employ this simple hackle guard.

SIZE OF BAND AND STRAW DEPEND ON FLY SIZE

LOOP IS BROUGHT FORWARD WHEN NEEDED TO BIND DOWN HACKLE.

KEEP LOOP END ON VISE WHEN NOT IN USE.

NATURAL BOBBIN THREADER

When you break your tying thread and can't find your threader, cut the broken thread with scissors so the end is not frayed, work the end into the bottom opening of your bobbin stem, put the tube end in your mouth and suck in quickly. If the bobbin tube isn't too gummed up with wax, you'll find this works like a charm.

POLY-PINCHER PLIERS

To help in the making of extended polypropylene fly bodies, here's a tool anyone can assemble at home. The brass can be purchased at any hobby shop. Using two sizes of triangular files results in different size grooves as illustrated.

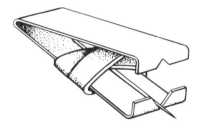

1. Materials needed:
- 1/2" X 6" brass strip
- Number 9 sewing needle
- Small rubber band

2. The rubber band should be wrapped on the pliers' large-grooved side, about 1" below the top bend.

3. Place needle butt under the rubber band so the point end extends about 3/8" beyond top bend. More extension will produce more poly to burn, resulting in a larger melted ball. Less protrusion is needed for small, thinner bodies.

4. Place polypropylene yarn in large V of the pliers, leaving about 1" of material on inside of pliers.

5. Close pinchers tightly to grasp poly, and wrap poly once around the needle, making sure poly encircles it.

6. Clip poly at the needle point.

7. Using a lighter, burn the poly that extends beyond the pliers. Check that the needle point is protruding from the center of the melted polypropylene.

8. Remove the poly, pull out needle, and insert tailing fibers into the hole left by the melted poly. Attach body to hook and complete the fly.

HAIR & HACKLE GUARD

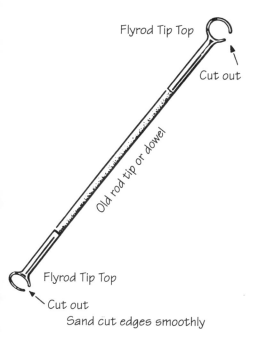

Flyrod Tip Top

Cut out

Old rod tip or dowel

Flyrod Tip Top

Cut out

Sand cut edges smoothly

Use this simple gadget when tying flies where spinning deer, or other body hair, is required. Simply slip this modified fly rod tip top over the head of the fly. Bring the thread through the gap and pull over the hair. This will hold the hair back so that tying off, before trimming, will be easier

After cutting out sections, and sanding, close gap in each tip top so there is just enough space for thread to pass between. By cutting out different size tip tops, a number of these can be made to use on different size flies.

THE VERSATILE SPLIT STRAW

Use a short section of plastic soda straw

as a hackle guard. This "split straw technique" of making of a longitudinal cut in the section of straw allows the tyer to slip it onto the tying thread, at the desired stage in the tying procedure, and then use it as a hackle guard to complete the head. The length of the straw varies from 1/8 inch upwards for use on flies of different sizes.

The split straw may also serve another purpose. Suppose the tyer wants to add to, or repair, that portion of the body just behind the hackle. If so, a split straw of the correct size is slipped over the body and pushed forward to hold the hackle down over the eye while the addition or repair is made.

NON-SLIP HACKLE PLIERS

Hackle pliers which afford a positive hold greatly assist fly tying efficiency. Pliers with sharp edges or rough gripping surfaces can devastate the fragile tips of prime feathers, whereas smooth surfaces often result in slippage, usually at an inopportune moment.

One solution is to spread open the pliers with a spacer. Apply a drop of barge (or Pliobond or similar adhesive) cement to each gripping surface, completely capsulating each jaw. Avoid excessive build-up to minimize bulk. Allow 8 hours of drying time, then apply talcum powder to relieve any tackiness. Wipe the powder free, release the spacer, and start tying with your most delicate hackle.

BOBBIN THREADERS

FUR-STRIP CUTTER

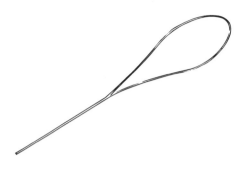

Use a floss threader to thread fly-tying bobbins. These floss threaders are designed for threading dental floss under bridges and between connected crowns. They are commonly available near the dental floss displays in drug store, K-Marts, and similar commercial outlets. The threaders are made of nylon and have enough stiffness to push the wax from the bobbin tube as they are passed through it with the thread. They are quite inexpensive and more satisfactory than the more expensive, commercially manufactured threading tools sold in many fly shops.

HANGING WHIP FINISHER

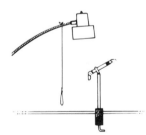

Any idea that saves time, saves money. A hanging whip finisher is just such an idea. It hangs from your tying lamp, or similar spot, and consists simply of a dental floss threader (mentioned above) connected to a long rubber thread of the sort used for bass bug or rubber spider legs. As a connector, use a plastic tube used in spinner making.

One of the problems in tying the effective Zonker flies is producing the necessary uniform fur strips. While these can be bought pre-packaged, it is far more economical to buy whole hides and dye them to the desired shades. To cut the strips, use an Olfa cloth cutter, available from most sewing stores. This tool looks like a scaled-down pizza wheel with an extremely sharp tungsten carbide wheel. By placing the hide fur side down on the cutting surface, and using a ruler as a guide, a large number of strips can be produced in a short time. The wheel is also effective for cutting latex, and is the best thing for splitting necks for dyeing. It should be equally effective on any thin sheet material.

Best of all, if you can persuade the sewer in your family to buy one, it can be borrowed at no cost, and you can save the money for that prize neck that you have been coveting.

SALT-WATER CUTTERS

Your nearest Radio Shack store will be pleased to sell you a "Radio Shack Wire Stripper" for about $2.50. This tool has adjustable V-notches in each jaw. Remove the stop so that the pliers will cut the wire leader material and you have a fine pair of salt water wire cutters. Inexpensive and if lost, easy to replace.

INTACT HACKLE

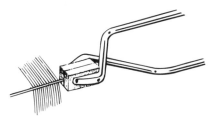

How can you keep hackle from breaking when using hackle pliers? From a rubber band (1/4" wide) cut two pieces as long as the inside of your hackle pliers jaws, and attach the pieces with Crazy Glue. The rubber surfaces hold the feather firmly but gently, and if you apply too much pressure, the worst that happens is that the feather will slip out of the jaws. This method will also permit the use of inexpensive hackle pliers that may have less than perfectly matched, smooth jaws.

BULLET HEADS

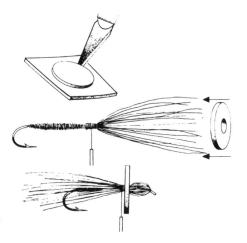

Having trouble tying a good bullet head on your Thunder Creek streamers or similar flies? Try this. Trace a circle the size of a penny on a piece of inner tube and cut out the circle. Using a leather punch, make a 1/16" hole in the center of the circle, and you're in business.

After the hair, elk, deer, or whatever, is tied in tight and the butts trimmed, let the bobbin and thread hang at the eye of the hook. Slip the rubber washer that you've made over the eye and push it back toward the bend of the hook, stopping when you get to the place where you want the head to stop. The thread is behind the washer, ready to wind and either half-hitch or whip finish. Remove the washer, lacquer the head thoroughly, and admire the perfect bullet shaped head you've tied!

REALLY CHEAP COMBINATION HALF-HITCH TOOL & HAIR PACKER

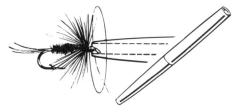

The best and cheapest half hitch tool is the body of a ball-point pen with the guts removed. It's smooth so the thread doesn't hang up or fray, and the hole is just large enough to slip over the eye of the hook. Whip finishing fly heads is great if you have enough room, but on a really tiny dry fly, three half hitches are more than enough to anchor the tying thread. Apply a tiny drop of head cement after you cut off the thread.

The other end of the pen barrel often has an opening of the proper size to be used as a hair packer to firmly pack the spun deer-hair bunches on the body of your bass bugs.

VELCRO MATERIALS HOLDER

An effective substitute for the common metal spring material clip found on most vises can be made by using the hook portion of a piece of Velcro, available at hardware, sewing, and chain stores. Velcro is sold in paired pieces, one piece is the hook, the other the eye. The material clip requires only the hook portion. Best of all, Velcro is now available with selfstick backing, making the installation of your new materials holder a cinch. Please note though, that the Velcro must be aligned so that the hooks are perpendicular to the axis of the vise jaws.

TEST CLIPS FOR HACKLE PLIERS

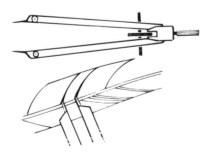

How about two pairs of guaranteed non-slip hackle pliers for under 2 dollars and about two minutes of your time? Go to your local Radio Shack and buy a card (2) of Archer Mini Test Clips. Lash a piece of rubber band about 1/16" wide and about 3/4" long to the shaft but under the copper clip with stout tying thread, and you're in business. After a year or so, the rubber band section will have to be replaced.

DRAFTSMAN'S DIVIDERS

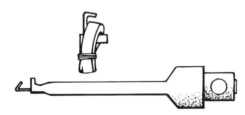

One of the handiest gadgets that a fly tyer can have on his bench is a pair of draftsman's dividers—the kind that

have an adjustment wheel between the points. By setting the dividers to 1 1/2 times the hook gape, the correct size of hackle can be selected by bending the stem of the feather over one point, and gauging the length of the fibres with the other point. The dividers are also useful for measuring equal widths of grasshopper wings, wet fly wings, and wing cases on nymphs. First, spray the quills with an adhesive spray such as Tuffilm, then pierce the feather near the stem with the divider points set to the desired width, and strip off equal quill segments. Other uses are adjusting the length of tails on your flies, sorting hooks, and cleaning the cement out of hook eyes.

HOME-MADE HAIR STACKER

Take an old lipstick container and clean it out. Place hair in the container, put the cover on, and proceed to tamp the hair. Remove the cover. By turning the base clockwise the hair will rise up so you can grasp it easily.

NON-SLIP HACKLE PLIERS

English style hackle pliers have a tendency to slip, especially at a crucial point in winding hackle. It helps to cover one of the jaws with a material that has some "give" to it, which seems to hold the hackle tip more securely. Heat-shrink tubing 1/16" diameter does the job nicely. This tubing is available at electronic supply stores. All you need is a piece 1/4" to 1/2" long, depending on the size of the pliers. Slip the tubing over the jaw and apply heat from a match. It will shrink tight to the jaw, and prevent the hackle from slipping or breaking when it is being wound.

CUTICLE CUTTERS FOR MATERIAL TRIMMING

When tying Atlantic-salmon flies as well as other complicated patterns, it is necessary to trim the waste ends of materials as precisely as possible. Usually sharp, fine pointed scissors are used. The problem is that if the blades are slightly dull the material will not be cut cleanly. Try a pair of cuticle trimmers that resemble very fine diagonal jawed wire cutters, but unlike wire cutters, the jaws meet almost parallel, closing at the tip first. Unlike scissors, even the heaviest tying material can be trimmed flush to the hook with these cutters. Although they cost almost as much as good scissors, they never need sharpening and have never failed to cut cleanly. There are a number of brands available at your drugstore.

STOP SLIPPAGE

Do you want an effective means to reduce slippage when using your conventional-style hackle pliers? Here's a suggestion that accomplishes this, and at the same time reduces breakage. Obtain some very fine emery cloth and simply glue two small pieces to the inside gripping surfaces of your hackle pliers. The fine abrasive surface of the emery greatly improves holding power, while the soft cloth edges prevent your hackle stem from being accidentally cut. The emery can be easily replaced when necessary.

SCISSOR TIPS

Tie a pair of scissors to each end of approximately four feet of cord, and

hang the cord around your neck. If you are right handed, hang these so that the fine scissors are on the right side with the heavy duty pair on the left.

As basic and elemental as this tip is it has the following advantages:
• Two pairs of scissors are always at hand
• No need to take your eyes off the work; simply grab the cord and find scissors
• Hands are free for material control, no need to cradle scissors while working
• No time is lost looking for the right scissors for the right job, or using fine scissors for heavy work when the heavier ones are lost amongst the clutter
• Scissors are out of the way when not needed
• Easy to locate, particularly for those of us who are forced to use a magnification aid (ever tried to find something when wearing or looking through a magnifier?)
• Probably best of all, you cannot drop and ruin your best scissors.

SCISSOR SHARPENING

Do you have an absolute favorite pair of scissors that has become dull and in need of sharpening? Are you wondering how to sharpen them yourself?

Don't do it! This is no job for amateurs and is best left to someone more experienced. Often your local fly shop will be able to advise you where they can be sent for proper sharpening.

MAGNETIC HELPERS
Magnets can be handy little things to have around your tying bench.

A small pocket-type magnet (looks like a pencil with a magnet instead of a lead) is useful for picking hooks or flies out of drawers, compartments or containers.

A magnetic "tool bar" available at almost any hardware store is useful for holding a supply of hooks, finished flies, and of course, tools such as needles, knives, English-style hackle pliers, etc.

And last, but not least, a larger magnet kept close by makes cleaning up that spilled box of hooks, or finding that one that dropped, a breeze.

USE AN OLD TOOTHBRUSH
A versatile tool can be made by trimming the bristles on an old toothbrush. The resulting gadget can be used as a dubbing teaser to rough up fly bodies, and also works well for removing the underfur from deer hair prior to spinning it.

VISE VERSATILITY

Try using a desk-top camera tripod for your fly-tying vise, and add dramati-

cally to its versatility. You eliminate the need for a heavy pedestal base and can set up anywhere.

EVERYMAN'S WING CUTTER
One alternative to an expensive set of wing cutters can probably be found in almost every household—a simple toe nail clipper. A good quality clipper will give you smooth, clean cuts to form upright cut wings for some mighty good looking mayfly duns.

NON-SKID PEDESTALS
Pedestal base vises are a blessing for the travelling tyer—no worries about whether the clamp will open wide enough to fit on a table, or if it does whether it will mar the table's surface. The only problem with pedestals is that if they are light enough to be reasonably portable, they are light enough to skid around on most tabletops they're sitting on. There are any number of ways around this problem; all involve gluing or cementing a layer of non-skid material to the bottom of the pedestal base. Sheet (gasket) cork, available at any automotive-supply store is one solution. Another is to use the round rubber feet that are used to prevent office machinery from moving around on the desk. (These usually have an adhesive on one side so they're easy to apply.) A piece of vinyl, cut from a drafting-table cover, and glued to the base works well, as do strips of rubber cut from an old inner tube. These are just a few of the materials that will make your vise non-skid.

HAND-HELD VISE
A great hand-held fly tying vise can be purchased at any arts and crafts store for about $1.00. It is sold as an X-acto knife, and once the blade is removed the jaws will hold any hook #8 or smaller. If you drill through the handle

at an angle and epoxy a long wood screw in the hole you've drilled, the vise can be used at streamside, too.

FROM THE SEWING STORE

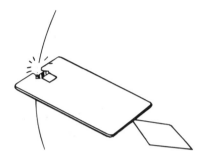

The handy gadget, manufactured by Dritz and shown here, costs only around one dollar at the local sewing store and is worth many times that at your fly tying bench. Use the very fine-wire threader as a whip finish tool and to clean excess head cement from the eye of the hook, and the other end to cut off the tying thread really close to the head.

NO-COST DUBBING BLENDER

Did you know that a 1/2 pound coffee can makes a great fur blender? Get yourself the fattest plastic drinking straw you can find and a 1/2 pound coffee can with a tight fitting lid. Poke a hole in the lid to fit the straw. Then poke a hole in the coffee can near the top, but below the lip of the lid. This hole should be about 3/16" in diameter; tape a piece of cheesecloth over it on the outside of the can. It will serve as a vent hole, so make certain the side of the lid clears it. Now put the colors of fur that you want to blend in the can and secure the lid. Insert the straw in the hole in the lid and blow like mad about a dozen times. The fur inside the can is going crazy, blending itself into the color that you want. The cheesecloth prevents bits of cut-up fur from scattering all over, and in just a minute or two you'll have a

good supply of dubbing. Best of all—the price is right!

IMPROVED HACKLEMASTER

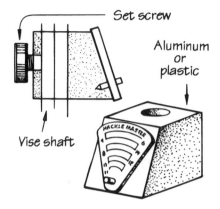

Al Troth's "Hacklemaster" is designed to be held in your vise jaws, enabling you to preselect the proper size of hackle. Many tyers like the gauge just fine, but not the pre-selecting procedure. You can make a device to hold the gauge on the shaft of your tying vise. Now if you need to check the hackle size, the gauge is instantly available, and when not in use, is out of the way.

PARACHUTE

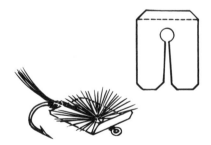

Use a piece of stiff plastic cut from a pocket calendar or the like, the width depending on the size of the fly you want to tie (usually 1/4 to 1/2 inch). Using a leather punch, cut a hole in the middle of the plastic piece, and then a tapered slot. Round off the edges and fold a 90° bend in the edge opposite the slot. Slide the hackle guard around the post and between the hackle and the body of the fly. Now you can tie off your hackle, put a bit more dubbing on the post, and whip finish without trapping any hackle barbules. Really a timesaver if you tie a lot of parachute flies, or:

BREAD WINNER

The small hard plastic tab that comes on a bag of English muffins makes a super guard when tying parachute hackle flies.

TEENY WEENY HAIR STACKER

For tying very small deer or elk hair flies here's a device that works better than the commercial stackers on the market—they're far to big for small quantities of hair. Your local stationery store will be pleased to sell you a container of replacement leads for a Pentel mechanical pencil. The plastic case is ideally suited as a stacker. This container is about 70 mm long and is diamond shaped, with inside dimensions of approximately 5 mm by 8 mm. Put in the elk hair butts down, replace the top and after a tap or two, the stacked hair is easily removed via the lid. The 0.5 mm lead container is the best as it is clear plastic with a black lid.

SAFETY FIRST
DUBBING NEEDLE

A dubbing needle or bodkin is one of the fly tyer's most useful tools, but it can inflict a nasty stab if picked up or stored carelessly. A .5 mm. Pentel or other mechanical pencil makes a safe alternative. Empty out all the lead and insert a small diameter needle (Dritz Quilting needles, size 10 work well) butt first into the hole at the tip of the pencil. The button on top of the pencil will advance and retract the needle as if it were lead, and the chances of stabbing yourself while reaching for another tool are greatly minimized.

UBIQUITOUS HALF-HITCH TOOL

There are certain flies - a #18 Little Black Stonefly comes immediately to mind - that have a head consisting of a small tuft of wing material brought forward to a point just over the hook's eye. This fly can be a major pain to tie off without the aid of a good half hitch tool. The tip of the thread bobbin is very similar in shape to a half hitch tool. With some practice to get the knack of it, you'll have one hanging in front of you all the time!

A HOT NEW FLY TYING TOOL

This gadget, an adaptation of an instrument used for eye surgery, is available at many bass fishing specialty shops for around ten or fifteen dollars and is called the "Wormizer Plastics Tool." What it does is provide flameless high temperatures to a very small area. Use it to melt monofilament ends when tying weedless hooks or nymph eyes, to burn away excess materials at the eye of the hook that are next to impossible to reach with scissors, to burn wings, to scoop out hollows for doll's eyes on bass bugs, and so on. This small hand tool is battery operated and there's no doubt that it's safer to use than an open flame, although care must still be exercised around solvents and flammable materials.

BETTER IS CHEAPER
(IN THE LONG RUN)

Other than your tying vise, a good pair of scissors will probably be your most costly investment as far as tying tools are concerned. Many authors and experts advise buying a second, inexpensive pair of scissors for cutting wire, tinsel, hard quills, etc., which besides dulling the blades often springs them out of alignment. The logic here seems to be that since you'll ruin the scissors cutting these materials anyway, you might as well spoil a cheap pair.

Surprisingly, little has appeared in books or articles promoting the use of a tool specifically designed for the purposes listed above. Any number of hand tool manufacturers include in their line a pair of small diagonal cutters. These tools are most frequently used in the electronics industry by both professionals and hobbyists. They are available in small, sharp-pointed and flush cutting styles, perfect for fly tying. They can be had in all price ranges depending on the level of quality desired, and even an inexpensive pair will outlast a dozen pairs of cheap scissors and do a lot better job as well.

WIRE CUTTER

Try using a leader nipper to cut wire, tinsel or lead. Not only will it save your scissors, but by sliding the nipper down until the jaws rest against the body of the fly, you'll get a neat flush cut, with no stub sticking out.

IMPROVING THE GINGHER NIPS

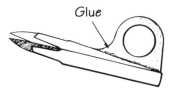

Glue

Thread nips are so much sharper than most fly-tying scissors that some tyers much prefer them. The Gingher brand is a favorite. The one big drawback is

that they don't come with a finger loop. Remedy this shortcoming as follows: From a 1/8" thick piece of clear acrylic drill a hole large enough to fit comfortably over your ring finger, and then cut the acrylic to shape on a band saw. A bit of sanding finishes it nicely, and then "superglue" it to the edge of the nips. The nice thing about making your own finger loop is that you can size it to fit your hand.

GLUE-GUN NYMPHS

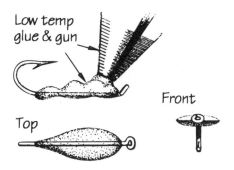

A low-temp glue gun is a handy gadget for the fly tyer. It can be used to make underbodies for flat-bodied nymphs. Here's how:

Place the hook into the tying vise (a rotary vise simplifies matters) and heat up the glue gun. Run a bead of glue on each side of the hook, building up the width of the body. Then run a bead on the top and bottom, connecting the glue already in place on the sides. Don't worry about making the body too wide or too thick. The glue never really hardens completely and can be cut with clippers or filed to the desired size and shape. Another good trick is to weight the hook with lead wire first, then run the glue over the lead, shaping it to the desired contour.

MAGNETIC ATTRACTION

A magnetized bodkin is extremely helpful when it comes to extracting one small hook out of a box. Rub the needle tip over a magnet a few times and there will be enough magnetic holding power to pick just one hook neatly away from its companions. But do not over-magnetize by rubbing over the magnet more than a few times. You'll wind up with a bodkin that will attract a dozen hooks at a time!

GODZILLA'S WING MEASURER

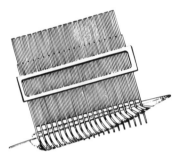

A carpenter's "copy-cat," used to transfer shapes of moldings, can be used to measure accurately the width of quill wings. Just press forward the pins that will give you the width required, press the tool into the feather and draw out. Spraying the quill first with clear lacquer helps hold the fibers together when you scissor them off the shaft.

GENERIC DUBBING TWISTER

An ordinary paper clip makes an excellent dubbing twister. Straighten out the clip, trim with wire cutters and bend the end into an open loop. You may prefer this tool to the more elaborate commercially available ones. And it's almost free, easy to make, and very comfortable to handle.

ALLIGATOR HACKLE PLIERS

Besides the test clips that are available at Radio Shack stores and which work well for hackle pliers, try the Micro Alligator Clips. At a cost of about $2.00 for a package of ten clips they can't be beat for price or utility.

CLIP TRICK

Tying wet flies and nymphs so that the hackle sweeps to the rear like it's supposed to is easy with this gadget, made from the ubiquitous paper clip. Straighten the paper clip, and using a pair of long-nose or round-nose pliers, make a loop in one end big enough to slip over the hook eye of your largest flies, and do the same on the other end, big enough to slip over the hook eye of your smallest. Don't close the loops completely - you want enough space for your tying thread to pass through as you move the tool past the eye to the front of the hackle. Holding the unused end of the tool, pull the hackle back and wind the thread against its base to hold the hackle in the nice swept back angle you've created.

DUBBING TWISTER

The tip of a small unused crochet hook makes a dandy dubbing twister when chucked into a pin vise. If you need a shorter model, tap the stub of the crochet hook into a 1 oz. bank type fishing sinker (remember those?).

HOOKS

"The hook must be thought of by the innovative fly tyer as the structural backbone of any fly he wishes to design."

Dave Whitlock
Fly Tyer, Summer 1978

BENDING HOOKS

If you should find it necessary to bend one of your fly tying hooks to achieve a special shape, you might discover that the tempering process has made your hook too brittle for bending, and that it breaks instead. This can often be overcome by removing the temper by heating the hook before bending it. By exercising a degree of care in the process it is often possible to remove the temper in the hook shank without significantly reducing the strength down toward the barb.

PRISTINE HOOKS

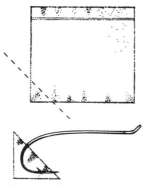

Often a hook will bear marks made by the jaws of the vise in which it was clamped. These marks do not seem to weaken the hook, and if it is a fly that will be fished, no problem. However, if you are tying a fly that is to be displayed, or a brooch pin, you'd not want to see any marks on the hook. To prevent them, cut the corner off a plastic bag and insert the bend of the hook into this "pocket" before you clamp the

hook into your vise. You'll finish up with an unblemished hook.

COCKEYED?

There are few things more annoying than discovering the eye of the hook defective or malformed on the fly that you've just finished. Make it a practice to look at the hook before you start to tie—is the eye properly closed? And is the eye the shape that its supposed to be? Most hooks are manufactured by machine by the mega-thousands so it's to be expected that a few imperfect ones will slip through. Better to find them before you tie your fly rather than after. If the fault is a slightly open loop often the hook can be used by building up a few windings of tying thread so as to fill the gap. If you don't do this your leader may fray and break on the stub end of hook wire.

IN PRAISE OF
THE LOOP-EYE HOOK

Except for very small flies, tying on a loop-eyed hook makes the positioning of wings about a zillion times easier. The two pieces of hook wire give a wider and more stable platform on which to tie hair or feather wings, so less thread is needed to hold the wing in position and the result is a smaller head. Another advantage of the return wire is that any possibility of roughness at the eye is eliminated, significantly reducing the possibility of the leader fraying. All up-eyed Atlantic-salmon hooks are formed with a loop eye; additional suggestions are the Mustad #9575 long-shank streamer hook and the Mustad #94863, an up-eye barbless hook available in sizes 8 through 14 and an excellent choice for Wulffs and Humpies as well as nymphs and wet flies. The Partridge CS2SH is a superb down-eye hook, available in black or silver, in sizes 2 through 8, and suitable for streamers and bucktails as well as steelhead patterns.

DEBARBING

If you've joined the growing ranks of catch-and-release fishermen, or if you like to make your sport even more of a challenge, you're probably fishing flies tied on barbless or debarbed hooks. The barbless ones cost significantly more than regular barbed hooks so many tiers opt to debarb their hooks. Should you debarb before or after the fly is tied? It just takes a second, while you're looking over the hook (point, eye, bend) to pinch the barb flat, then clamp it in the vise and tie away. This also avoids the possibility of breaking the hook after having tied your fly.

PRESHARPENING

Try sharpening each hook before you put it into your vise. There's less possibility of ruffling a newly-tied fly, or messing up the not-quite-dry head cement by sharpening it before rather than after.

HOOK I.D.

Although boxes of hooks are identified on the cover by number and size, an example of what's inside can be provided by fastening a sample to either the end or the cover of the box with a piece of transparent tape. This makes hook selection easier when you can't remember all those model numbers.

SHARPENING SMALL HOOKS

Some tyers prefer to flatten barbs and sharpen hooks before starting to tie. Sharpening is made easier by mounting the hook in the vise upside down and then honing it to a triangular point. Almost any sharpener will work on hooks down to size 14 or so, but when the hooks are in the size 18 and smaller range, their gape is too small for most sharpeners. A trip to the local woodworking shop can provide you with a small India slip stone, normally used to sharpen woodworking chisels and gouges. It is made by Norton Manufacturing Company and has a catalog number of MS-42. It cost around $5.00. It is small—2 1/4" by 7/8" and one edge tapers down small enough to easily fit the gape of even the smallest hook.

HOOK RETRIEVAL

By placing a small magnet in the bottom of your Wastrol or similar waste container at your tying area, any hooks that are accidentally swept into the trash can be retrieved. With the cost of hooks steadily rising, this is a good way to make sure that you use all the hooks you've paid for.

JOINING HOOKS ON TANDEM FLIES

Many tandem flies use stainless-steel wire to join the two hooks together. Stiff wire does not allow the rear hook to move much for a natural appearance. Instead, use a length of 15-pound Maxima monofilament. It allows the rear hook more motion, but it has a tendency to pull out.

A solution is to melt a premeasured length of 15-pound line by holding each end close to the bottom of the flame of a match. A small solid bump is formed which, when bound on a hook, will not pull out—even when trolled over a snag!

The light mono allows the flies to swim in a more natural side-to-side motion, and seems to be plenty strong.

AN EASY WAY TO PICK UP HOOKS

To pick up small hooks magnetize your tying scissors. They will easily pick up hooks as large as size 8. To magnetize them simply stroke the back of the cutting blades about 20 times with a permanent magnet from a cabinet magnetic latch. Stroke both blades with the same side of the magnet from the wide part to the tip and they are set for years of help picking up small hooks right out of the box or out of a pile of feathers or dubbing on the bench.

SPILLED HOOKS

Dropping a box of very small trout hooks can be a costly and messy mistake. Placing a small magnet inside the box will keep the hooks together just in case this ever happens.

VISE DE-BARB HOOKS

Using barbless hooks for fly fishing is becoming very popular. If you don't have some flat pliers handy here's a quick and easy way to debarb a hook

without having to buy barbless hooks in various styles and sizes.

Before tying the fly, put the hook point sideways into the jaws of the vise and close them gently. The barb will be flattened neatly, and you can tie a fly on the hook.

Most quality vises with fine jaws can bend barbs on hooks down to size 20. Don't, however, go so far as to damage the vise jaws when using very large hooks.

CLEANING HOOK EYES

Most tyers use a bodkin to clean the head cement out of the hook eye. This tool does at best an indifferent job—far more satisfactory is the use of a piece of hackle stem. Simply insert the bottom of the hackle stem in the eye and pull through. The barbs act as a sponge for the surplus lacquer, and the result is a really clean and unclogged eye.

STAINLESS KEEL HOOKS

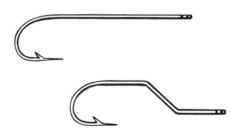

For weedless saltwater flies a Mustad #34011 hook can be bent to keel hook shape! Use two pairs of pliers, or put the hook in a vise and use one pair of pliers to bend it to the desired.

LOOK BEFORE YOU TIE

Examine the hook carefully before you insert it into the jaws of the vise. Look for the following flaws: malformed or improperly closed eye, badly formed barb, blunted or bent point, twisted shank. It is maddening to discover only after the fly is tied that the hook is faulty.

PICKING UP TINY HOOKS

Problem: how do you extract very small hooks, one at a time, from the confines of the boxes in which they are purchased? Solution: with jeweler's forceps. These instruments are very-finely pointed stainless-steel tools capable of picking up the most minute object. They are available with both straight and curved tips. You may also want to carry one in your fishing vest, finding it valuable for extracting small dry flies from fly boxes without mashing wings or hackle. The forceps can be found at swap meets and other places where scissors, used dental tools and the like are available to the general public.

BENDING HOOKS

Sometimes it is desirable to modify the bend of a hook, either to increase its hooking capability or to make it less of a weed catcher. Rather than using pliers, which sometimes scars the hook wire or increases the brittleness of the wire as you usually don't get it right on the first attempt, try this. By pounding two nails about 3/4" or an inch apart into a board or your tying table, you'll have a convenient bending jig for hooks. It is a simple matter to either open up the gape or modify the shape of the shank.

HEADS, THREADS, BOBBINS & SPOOLS

"If rods and reels are the body of tackle, then flies have to be its poetic soul. They are the embodiment of an historically derived aesthetic, unique to any sport, the manifestations of theories of fishing and a window onto the trading tradition of the nations where they were made."

Harmon Henkin
Fly Tackle, 1976

KEVLAR THREAD

One of the super-strong threads in the market is made of fibers of a material called Kevlar. For large saltwater streamers or for bass bugs the unusual strength of this thread seems perfect—grab a piece and try to break it. Be careful, you might cut yourself before it breaks. But make a simple overhand knot in the thread and it breaks easily. You might keep this weakness in mind as you use this thread on your flies.

TABBING AN ELASTIC BAND

Trying to grasp the elastic band that most of us use to keep a spool of tippet material from unwinding is a real pain unless the band has a tab or "ear" on it. However, if you tie a granny knot in a rubber band, voilà—now you have an easy to grasp tag.

BREAKING THREAD

Probably the most common complaint of beginning (and some not-so-beginning) tyers is that they break the tying thread. The best way to learn how not to do this is to deliberately and slowly break the thread so as to learn just how much pressure can be applied safely. The breaking strengths of tying threads vary considerably by manufacturer and by size, so this is not a meaningless exercise. Place a hook in the vise of the size you will use with a particular thread, attach the thread, and apply pressure. Your muscles will soon learn just how

heavy handed to be to attach materials to the hook without breaking the thread.

BOBBIN THREAD ANCHORS

One of the petty annoyances of fly tying is having the bobbin thread fall out of the bobbin tube. This usually happens when you've finished tying and are cleaning up the area. At the end of your tying session try clipping your hackle pliers to the end of the tying thread. Not only can't the thread fall out of the tube, but the hackle pliers are easy to locate when you start your next tying session.

USED SPOOLS

Save your old spools from tying threads. Wind on wool, angora, mohair, or other yarns and flosses. Use a bobbin with a large tube and a flare tip. Using the bobbin will save material, time, and will prevent your hands from soiling the materials.

FOR HEAVIER FLOSS

Any single-strand floss can be made into three-strand with a minimum of

41

effort. You'll need access to a sewing machine, three spools of the single strand, a 2" or 3" piece of plastic tubing (a drinking straw will do), and an empty bobbin. Put the bobbin on the bobbin winder of the sewing machine; insert the dowel or pencil through the holes in the spools, and the ends of the floss through the straw or tubing. Then pull enough of all three strands off the spools to attach to the bobbin, and s-l-o-w-l-y wind the gathered floss strands onto the bobbin. Using the straw or plastic tube to guide the floss onto the bobbin prevents pressure from your fingers from fraying the material. Interestingly enough, one bobbin holds three full spools of single strand!

STICKY SPOOLS?

How about when you put a new spool of thread in your bobbin? The previous, almost empty spool, fed out thread smoothly. Now, the new full spool, sticks, binds and skips as you wrap another fly. Bobbin adjustments don't help. It is very annoying.

Here is a simple solution. Rub a stub of an old wax candle around the holes in the thread spool. It works as a lubricant. The thread will now feed out very smoothly.

Just be sure to use dry candle wax, and not dubbing wax. That would gum up everything for sure.

HOW TO TIE A COMPLEX PATTERN WITH A RIDICULOUSLY SMALL HEAD

There are many techniques employed to ensure the smallest possible head on salmon flies, sometimes to the point of being disproportionate to the size of the fly. However, here is a technique suggested in an English book. Assemble all the components for the wings. Construct them and tie onto a bare hook. Varnish the head and set aside until

thoroughly dry, and then apply a second, heavy coat of varnish. Let dry. Dress the body on a second hook and set aside. Carefully cut through the varnished head holding the wing on the first hook from underneath and carefully slide off the wings (the head will form an inverted "U"). Slip this inverted "U" over the bodied hook just in front of the throat and take a careful turn or two of thread immediately behind the original head. Use just enough thread to hold the wings in position. Keeping plenty of tension on the thread, scrape away the old head with the point of a small sharp knife. When all the varnish and thread have been removed, work some fresh varnish into the exposed butts of the wings, and whip finish. All the components of the wing are now tied in together instead of one at a time. The result is an extremely small head.

NEAT HEADS

For small, smooth, strong, nice-looking heads on your flies, always whip finish with your wraps progressing from the fly body towards the hook eye. Going the other way makes the wraps pile one on top of the other, causing a lumpy head, and more important, fewer wraps of thread hold the trimmed end. By wrapping towards the hook eye, the first thread wrap to be pulled tight is the one closest to the eye, with subsequent wraps progressing back towards the body. The result is a smooth, nicely tapered head with the thread end well protected by each individual wrap.

CHENILLE BOBBIN

Do you waste inches of material when tying chenille/floss/lead or other stuff that is supplied on cards? To control as well as conserve, cut or punch two holes in the top of the card and insert one end of the material through each hole in turn. Allow enough material through the holes to complete the fly you're working on. The card then becomes, more or less, a bobbin. You may then tie in the material and let it hang (it will not drop or unwind), and when finished, you can snip off the material at the hook, thereby avoiding any waste.

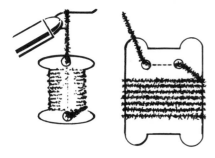

DOUBLE STRENGTH

While tying bass bugs, saltwater patterns or spinning deer hair, fly tyers often encounter the problem of running out of 4/0 or larger thread, and breakage when a substitute is used. Prewaxed nylon will break if too much pressure is applied and Monocord also has its limitations.

By pulling off twice as much thread as you need and attaching both ends to the hook shank, you have double-strength thread capable of withstanding heavy tying.

You may need to spin with hackle pliers and wax to ensure cohesion of this double strand.

SEWING SUPPLIES

Sometimes it is hard to find just the right item from regular fly-tying sources—try combing sewing and yarn shops for goodies.

Fine oval and gold tinsels are found in Singer Sewing Centers under the trade name Talon. Evidently it is Mylar over a nylon core. It's strong, doesn't tarnish, and comes on spools that fit a standard bobbin.

For protecting the colored thread bodies on midge larvae and pupae patterns, even the narrowest Swannundaze was too coarse. Again, in the Singer shop you will discover Invisible Sewing Thread. It's strong, doesn't coil, has no memory, and is quite elastic. Wound over a colored thread body it adds a nice sparkle without masking the color, and resists damage from sharp teeth.

TAMING TINSELS AND FLOSS

Flosses and tinsels have a nasty habit of coming unwound from their spools and then the materials become dirty, frayed, twisted or crumpled. In order to avoid this waste spend a few minutes making this spool holder from a transparent plastic film canister. Several brands of 35 mm. film (Fuji and Konica) are sold in these cannisters. You'll need as many as you have spools to protect, plus some Styrofoam trays that supermarkets use to package meats. Cut a lengthwise slot in the side of the cannister about 1" long and about 1/8" wide. An Exacto knife works well for this. In order to fit the spool firmly in the cannister, cut four circles the diameter of the container (use the end of it as a template) from the Styrofoam and force two of them to the bottom of the cannister. Thread the floss or tinsel out through the slot, insert spool, add one or two more Styrofoam discs, and replace cover. Cut a slit in the cover to anchor the loose end of the floss or tinsel. Works well, doesn't it?

THREAD CONTROL

A right-handed tyer will generally bring the thread toward his body, then up and over the hook. This action puts a certain twist in the thread. When using a soft loop to tie in tails, this twist causes the loop to flip up toward the eye of the hook instead of back toward the fingers of the left hand. To correct this problem, let the bobbin dangle and give it a counterclockwise spin (as viewed from above). Spinning a dubbing loop counterclockwise causes the dubbing wraps to lie tightly together on the hook shank. When holding antennae in the right hand at the eye of the hook, and wrapping the thread with the left, you want the soft loop to move toward the hook eye, so spin the bobbin clockwise.

THREAD & BOBBIN STORAGE

The storage of bobbins filled with tying thread can turn into a tangled situation. A plastic book binding strip can cure this problem at minimal cost. By cutting off each ring with a pair of scissors, and then cutting a 1/4" slit in one end, you have a bobbin cover that works very well. It is simply wrapped around the bobbin and the thread is secured in the slit. About 20 covers can be made from each strip, which only costs about 50 cents at almost any printing shop. The strips are made in various diameters to fit different size spools.

NEAT HEADS

If you are occasionally guilty of that hasty whip finish that picks up some hackle barbs or fur debris, here's a solution. Using a set of Thompson Hackle Guards, and a butane cigarette lighter will instantly remedy the problem. Place the proper size guard (they come in sets of three) over the eye of the hook, exposing the fuzzy head. A quick singe with the lighter will remove the debris and leave a clean, neat head, ready for lacquering. On small flies, if you use waxed tying thread, the burst of heat will seal the thread, eliminating the need for head cement.

NEAT SPOOLS

Many sewing or notions stores carry a product called "Thread Locks," made by Nancy's Notions, Ltd., P.O. Box 683, Beaver Dam, WI 53916. These handy little widgets are flexible plastic buttons designed to be inserted into the end of a spool to trap the loose end of sewing thread. They work just as well for fly-tying materials. Some of our material spools may require a slight and easily performed modification in order to ensure a snug fit into the end of the spool. Slice the tube part of the button with a razor blade, splay out the two halves, and the Thread Lock will now stay in place.

Using them could not be simpler—just wrap the loose end of thread around the tip of the button and then insert. For bulkier materials, lay the tag end across the hole in the spool and then insert the button. The wasteful tangle will be gone forever—no more uncoiled wire, tinsel, floss and thread.

SMOOTH SPOOLS

Most fly tyers will agree that it's almost impossible to fault the design and utility of a Matarelli or similar type of wire thread bobbin. Yet we use an object of questionable quality with it—the plastic spool on which thread is sold. Mold flash, burrs, and any number of other abnormalities typically plague the center hole of the spool, causing it to drag in the bobbin or to not run smoothly. Maybe that's why tying thread breaks so often!

The solution is to apply a small square cut from a roll of PTFE (Teflon) thread sealing tape to each end of the spool prior to placing it in the bobbin. This stuff is sold by the roll in the plumbing department of any hardware store, and each roll contains 520 inches of the stuff, so you'll have plenty on hand. It is much easier to use the tape than to try to taper and smooth the margins of the center hole, and much neater than using some sort of grease or lubricant in an effort to make a spool run smoothly.

REDUCE CUT THREADS

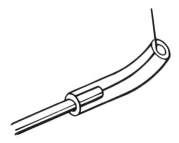

If the edge of your bobbin starts cutting your thread, purchase a small length of soft plastic tubing, outside diameter about one-eighth inch, from any surgical supply store. Slide a small section over the tip of your bobbin and allow to extend about one half inch beyond the tip of the bobbin. This will prevent any cutting of the thread.

BOBBINS REDUX

One of the most common complaints in all of fly tying is bobbin tubes that cut or fray the tying thread. The damage may be a nick or nicks at the tip of the tube, or the grooving may run down the inside diameter of the tube.

To repair the first problem you'll need to have at hand the following materials: 320-grit emery cloth, preferably used, a small piece of heavy hide such as elk, a bit of jeweler's rouge or buffing compound, and a length of heavy cotton twine. Press the damaged end of the thread tube down on the emery paper and rotate the tube back and forth until it is fairly smooth. Next, repeat the same spinning motion with the tube pressed into the hide, on which you have put a light layer of the abrasive compound. The final polish is put on the lip of the tube by applying a bit of the rouge or polishing compound (or in a pinch, Bon Ami) to the twine, and pulling it back and forth inside the tube until the lip is smooth, polished, and burr-less.

In the case of a heavily grooved tube, the best method is to grind the tube back to a point where all the grooving has been removed, making certain that you have a true right angle when finished with this first step. Next, take a small metal-cutting drill with a diameter approximately that of the tube, and by hand, break the inside edge of the tube. Then proceed as for repairing a nicked tube.

Another method of removing nicks is to use a round wooden toothpick or bamboo skewer. Dip the end of the toothpick or skewer in a bit of Bon Ami, Comet, or jeweler's rouge and press it into the tube, and spin it, using only a minimum amount of pressure. Slow and easy is the way to go, so as not to make the problem worse.

SUPERIOR HACKLE GUARD

Fingers make pretty good hackle guards but then you're left with only one hand to work on the fly. The arrangement I'm going to tell you about keeps the hackle, or wings, or whatever, out of the way, but leaves both hands free. Your local Radio Shack store will be happy to sell you a package of heat shrink tubing in a variety of diameters. A 1 to 2 inch section of 1/4" tubing slipped over the tube of your bobbin before you attach the thread to the hook will ride on the tube, out of your way, until you want to trim, or glue or whatever without the hackle or wing getting in the way. It's a matter of a moment to slide the tube off the bobbin and over the head of the fly, do whatever trimming or lacquering you want, and then remove the hackle guard to its resting place on the bobbin tube.

WAX FOR NEAT SPOOLS
Some spools of thread come with a notch for anchoring the thread when not in use. But not all spools! When you buy one that doesn't, here's an easy way to prevent the thread from unwinding. When you remove the thread from the bobbin put a little - it doesn't take much - dubbing wax on the end of the thread and stick it to the spool. When you use that spool again, clip off the end of thread with the wax to pre-

vent the dubbing wax from clogging the bobbin tube.

BOBBIN TENSION

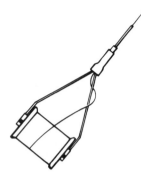

A simple way to add a little more tension to your tying thread is to loop the thread around one leg of the bobbin. This enables you to tie your flies using as much tension as the thread will take, and also prevents the bobbin from drifting downward when hanging free. A more durable fly results due to the increased and consistent tension on the tying thread.

WHIP FINISHES

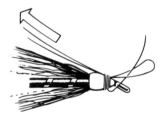

Many beginning tyers have all sorts of trouble with the infamous but very necessary whip finish. Here's a simple way to tie it. Cut off about a 4 inch piece of tying thread, preferably of a different color than the head color of your fly, and make a loop. Place the loop of thread over the fly head, the fold facing the head of the fly, and wrap over both ends four or five times. Cut the tying thread, leaving about a 3" tag. Insert the tag end of the tying thread through the loop that you've laid in and pull the cut ends of the loop. This will bring the end of the tying thread under itself, which is what a whip finish is. This is the same process that's used to finish off fly rod guides.

HANDLING KEVLAR THREAD

This stuff has found extensive use for making spun deer hair bodies because of its amazing strength. However, rather too easily it can cut through the hair that you are trying to attach. A solution to this problem is in Dick Talleur's book, *The Versatile Fly Tier*. Simply spin the bobbin to remove most of the twist in the thread before tying in the deer hair. This increases the thread's diameter at the tie-in point, and greatly reduces the chance of the thread severing the hair.

REDUCING THREAD INVENTORIES

Instead of stopping to change the color of the thread in your bobbin, use only white thread, but have on hand a selection of waterproof marking pens in the colors of the threads that you're replacing. It takes only a second to run the pen up and down the thread - lots quicker than pulling out the old thread, hunting for the bobbin threader, finding the new spool, etc., and certainly less expensive than buying a lot of bobbins. Once the fly head is lacquered, it's impossible to tell that you've dyed your thread.

REJUVENATING SPOOLS

Many of our fly-tying materials come on plastic spools, most of which have burrs and mold marks on them that snag and fray the material. Trying to smooth these rough spots with a knife blade seems only to exacerbate the problem. Try heating an Exacto blade and melting these troublesome areas.

EMERGENCY

The next time your thread breaks in the middle of tying a fly, instead of watching the fly unravel while you rethread your bobbin, simply clamp the broken thread or loose material in your hackle pliers. Everything will be immobilized on the hook shank, giving you plenty of time to rethread and restart.

WAXLESS BOBBIN TUBES

I'm sure that every fly tyer has had the problem of wax buildup in the bobbin tube. This can easily be removed by inserting a bobbin threader into the tube and then, instead of inserting the end of the tying thread into the threader loop, sliding in a piece of paper towel about the size of a dime. Slowly pull the threader back through the tube, and the towel will remove the built up coating of wax.

MATERIALS
SELECTIONS & SUBSTITUTES

"Fly-making is a fascinating amusement, and we wish that it was not so difficult to obtain first-class materials for artificial flies. No one can turn out a perfect fly with indifferent hackles and feathers."

Theodore Gordon
in *Fishing Gazette*, 1903

SELECTING HACKLE

DRY FLY
HACKLE

SPADE
HACKLE

STREAMER
HACKLE

When selecting hackles, particularly from hybrid capes such as Metz, Hoffman and Hebert, take care to choose feathers not only for barb length, but also for thickness and length of stem (also known as shaft). Shorter feathers with generally thicker stems will be to the sides of the cape; longer feathers with narrower stems will be toward the middle. You will find those near the sides (adjacent to the spade feathers) most useful for a palmered hackle fly, such as an elk-hair caddis. They will be of adequate length and have more durable stems appropriate to that use. However, they are not as useful for standard dry flies such as Adams, Cahills and Wulffs due to their length as well as their coarser stems. The feathers toward the middle of the cape have the length, stem shape and diameter that are more suitable for hackling the dry fly.

BUILT-UP BODIES

When building up bodies on nymphs or streamers, unwaxed dental floss is superior to anything else. For flat-bodied nymphs, simply tie lead wire on each side of the hook, and then wrap over the wire with dental floss. You can then flatten the body even more with smooth faced pliers. The floss can be colored with Pantone pens, or mottled, and then overwrapped with clear Swannundaze to form a very durable and lifelike fly.

FUN WITH FOAM

Use your imagination and experiment with some of the many possible applications of closed-cell foam. Some ideas you might start with include: an all foam ant, a floating caterpillar made like a wooly worm, Humpies using the foam to replace the deer or elk back, grasshopper bodies, injured minnow imitation—virtually anything that floats. Steelheaders and salmon fishermen might want to include foam in their "damp" or skater patterns.

MAKE YOUR OWN WINGS

An amazing variety of fly-tying products can result from your taking scissors and waterproof markers and applying them to that super-tough Tyvec material of which many envelopes are made. Tyvec converts into some realistic, and almost indestructible, shell-backs, wing cases, and down wings.

FLYLINE RECYCLING

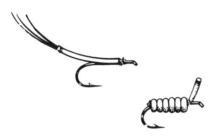

Old floating flyline can be used to construct the bodies for extended-body mayflies. Cut a section of flyline and strip the coating from each end. Stretch this section between two fly-tying vises and using thread wraps attach your preferred tailing material at one end of the coated portion. Once cemented, remove the flyline from the vise, cut away the excess by the tail, and cut the new fly body to the appropriate length.

Some tyers make grasshopper and stonefly bodies by wrapping the flyline around the hook shank.

POPPERS UNDERFOOT

Fly tyers will look anywhere for sources of materials. Take, for example, multi-colored beach sandals with soles constructed from several layers of laminated closed-cell foam. By cutting various size cylinders from the sole you obtain a supply of potential bass or panfish popper bodies that are quite durable.

TINSEL ALTERNATIVE

If you're having difficulty locating oval tinsel in fine and extra-fine sizes, and don't like the price and fragility when you do find it, try using a strand of fine wire for tinsel tags, and twisting two or three strands of the wire together for the ribbing. Not only is this wire inexpensive, it's very easy to find, and available in silver, gold or copper. It is easy to work with, and it's far more durable that the material it's replacing. In order

to spare your scissors, though, use the back part of the blades to cut the lengths you need.

FEATHER PRESSING

Occasionally, in an unguarded moment, a tyer will buy a chicken neck on which the feathers have excessive curve, making them all but unusable for streamer wings. This curvature can often be removed by pressing the feathers under a damp cloth with a medium hot iron.

PRISMATIC STREAMERS

Prismatic tape, found in most auto parts stores, can enhance the flash and attractiveness of streamers.

The metallic tape comes in a variety of colors, and creates a rainbow of prism colors much more lifelike than standard tinsels.

FOR STIFFER TAILS

When selecting some hackle barbs to serve as tails on your dry flies you are usually seeking relatively long and stiff fibers. On a rooster neck there are some shorter feathers, found at both the extreme outside edges of the neck, which are called "spade hackles." These feature barbs which are most suitable as a tailing material.

LATEX-LIKE

There is a new type of rubber glove being used by the medical profession lately. They are not the same as the latex kind you have probably already cut up for tying material. They are made of a more plastic-like material than the rubbery latex.

Strips of these gloves can be used in the same way as latex in tying flies. The material has some different features that make it worth trying.

The stuff is stronger, does not stretch as much as latex, and is slightly thicker. It is easier to cut straight with a razor blade and rule. It is also almost clear, without the tan tone of latex, easily colored with any type waterproof marker, and is resistant to most solvents.

MENDING JUNGLE COCK EYES

The importation of jungle-cock necks has been illegal for a number of years now, so those that occasionally turn up are not usually of very good quality—many of the nails are split, and the colors in the "eyes" are pale. Split jungle-cock nails can be repaired and the color enhanced in several ways.

1. Using any good waterproof glue, preen the splits together with your fingers. Then back each nail with tissue paper. When dry, trim any protruding corners of tissue.

2. Place a drop of Pliobond cement on a piece of paper. Holding the nail by the stem, pull it through the Pliobond, good side up, until the splits come together. Lightly stroke the splits together with your fingers, and place the repaired nail on a piece of waxed paper to dry.

3. Buy a small bottle of pure orange shellac and a tiny brush. Apply a bit of shellac to the split feather, and with light pressure from thumb and forefinger, stroke the wet shellac through the feather until the drying shellac makes pulling difficult. This should draw the split together, but very deep splits on large nails may need a little further adjustment. This method not only mends the splits, but adds color and brightness to less than prime quality feathers. The late Col. Joseph E. Bates suggested this method.

4. Take a black body feather slightly smaller than the jungle-cock tip you want to fix. Using your finger, rub it full of fly head cement and let it dry. Next give it a light coat of cement on one side and press it against the underside of the jungle-cock feather you want to seal. Work the splits in the jungle cock together. They will be cemented shut and stick to the body feather.

TUBING-CORE WINGS
Some of the cores found in braided Mylar tubing are a synthetic sparkle yarn that can be used to wing dry flies— either duns or spinners. This yarn can be dyed or barred with waterproof marking pens, and it floats beautifully. It is also a good substitute for bucktail.

FLY TYING WIRE
A broken radio, clock or almost any electric motor with an electromagnet can be a source for small-diameter copper wire that is ideal for fly tying. The wire will often be enameled in useful colors such as red, green, brown, or black, or its natural finish may be used.

SILKWORM GUT SUBSTITUTE
Tyers who enjoy dressing the classics, complete with gut eyes or snells have had a difficult time of late as the supply of silkworm gut has all but vanished. Here is a more than adequate substitute, using monofilament and a hair dryer. Cut 3 or 4 strands of 4 to 6 pound test mono, knot the strands together at one end, carefully even the strands, and knot the other end. Clamp one knot in your vise, and with a dubbing twister or shepherd's crook twist the strands of mono tight. With the drier set on "high," slowly run it along the mono strands. Continue to apply heat until

the twists stay when you let go of the twister. Repeat this step three times, or until the mono remains twisted when you release your grip. The result is surprisingly like silkworm gut, and adds a period "look" to your classic dressings.

PAINT-BRUSH TAILS

Some artists paint brushes have synthetic bristles that make ideal tailing material for dry flies. The best seem to be the brushes with white or natural colored fibers designed for use with acrylic paints . These can be dyed to the shade you desire. It's very convenient to simply pick up a paintbrush and select 2 or 3 perfect fibers, all the same size. The brush doesn't get lost in the clutter on your table, either!

JUNGLE-COCK EYES

Imitation jungle-cock eyes may be fabricated from easily obtained feathers, and any of these methods result is a much more satisfactory product than the plastic eyes available at suppliers.

1. Starling feathers are fragile, but by backing them with stronger feathers (hen hackle, for example) and trimming off any hen hackles barbules that protrude, and then coating the package with shellac or Pliobond for strength, they are not bad substitutes for the real thing.

2. The body feathers of guinea fowl, the ones with the large dots, can, with a minimum of hassle, be made to look very like jungle cock. Leave the rows of dots next to the stem white, but then color the second row out with a yellow marker.A couple of coats of head cement or clear nail polish over the feather, and you're ready to cut out a couple of slips for use as cheeks on any pattern you choose. These fake jungle-cock nails really dress up streamers and salmon flies and they don't cost

an arm and a leg!

3. Still another method is to use black hen hackle trimmed to the appropriate shape. With white and yellow hobby enamel, paint on the "eyes". When thoroughly dry, apply several coats of "Tuffilm", shellac, or head cement to give your substitute jungle cock the shiny appearance of the real thing.

4. A segment of barred-woodduck-flank feather (the lemon colored feather with a distinct black and white tip) can prove to be an attractive substitute when used in place of natural jungle cock. Some tyers have also used sections of golden pheasant tippets for the same purpose.

Some of the above methods are time consuming, but one evening spent in creating "jungle cock" will supply enough for months of tying.

KIDDIE'S BALLOONS

A package of children's balloons provides an inexpensive source of colored latex for nymph patterns. They are easy to cut into strips and the colors may be varied by changing the tension as you wrap the strip. Particularly useful are the greens, pinks, reds and yellows found in almost every package. Try the green balloons for caddis nymphs. And the ones you don't use, you can inflate and give to the kids!

TANNING WITHOUT TEARS

If you've ever been presented with an entire deer or elk hide by a well-meaning friend who figures that his gift is good for a lifetime supply of your flies, you know what a mess trying to tan the hide at home can be. All this may be changing with the introduction by Tandy Leather Corp. of a product called "Tannit." Here's how to proceed.

Scrape off as much of the fat and membrane from the flesh side of the hide as you can and salt it with non iodized salt. Roll up the hide and leave overnight. Next day scrape the flesh side one more time, then wash the hide well in order to remove all the salt and dirt from it and squeeze out as much water as possible. This step is more easily accomplished if the hide is first cut into manageable pieces. Mix the Tannit according to the directions and apply it to the flesh side when the hide is warm. Fold the hide flesh side to flesh side and leave it to cure overnight.

Next day unfold the hide and stretch it by pulling on it from all the edges. This works the Tannit deep into the skin. Continue to pull the hide until it is dry. The length of time necessary to completely cure a hide depends on the animal—rabbits take only a day or so, raccoons three or four days and elk as much as two weeks.

MOOSE MANE

This stuff is surely one of the most versatile of all fly-tying materials. It is readily available, durable, flexible enough under water to give a bit of movement to the fly, available in two colors, and long enough for almost any use. Here are just a few of the uses: tails, bodies, wing cases and legs on small nymphs, and hopper legs. Knot bundles

of moose mane hairs for legs on larger flies, stone fly nymphs, for example. To make the knot in the leg, use either your dubbing needle, or a very small crochet hook.

CORK BODIES

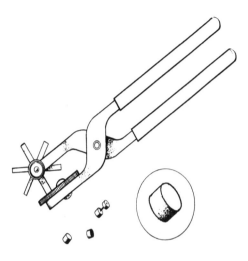

Wheel-type leather punches make great cork-bodied terrestrials. Slice your cork cylinder into the desired width, and punch out using the desired diameter of punch. The resulting cork cylinders need no sanding. Thread two "punch-outs" on a length of monofilament, burn the ends of the mono, and put a drop of magic glue on each end of the mono where it meets the cork body sections. Lacquer with the desired color and secure to the hook. Two sections make ants of any size. Three or more make worms, caterpillars, etc. Build an insect. Works with sheets of closed-cell foam as well.

SARAN-WRAP WINGS

Experiment with wet-fly and dry-fly wings made of Saran wrap, poly bags or any of the similar translucent packaging materials commonly found in the kitchen. We've found that all sorts of upwing and downwing patterns can be constructed using these materials, some of which are easily tinted using waterproof magic markers. For a highly realistic imitation use sandpaper to lightly etch lines that resemble the veins of a natural insect's wing.

HERON SUBSTITUTE

No doubt about it, there's been a resurgence in tying Spey type flies. They make excellent steelhead and salmon flies, with lots of movement in the water to tempt a fish. The problem is that heron, which is the feather called for in these dressings, is unobtainable by legal means, and the usual substitutes are too short for large size 1/0 and 3/0 hooks. The answer? Prime marabou blood feathers, with long fine tips, tied in tip first, either the entire feather, or with one half stripped away, depending on the sparseness of your dressing. Once the feather is secured, take a small amount of extra-hold styling mousse and stroke it into the feather, then pick each strand apart from its neighbor with your bodkin and continue to stroke the feather until dry. You'll end up with what appears to be real heron. Until the fly is wet, the marabou will stay this way, so it's a good solution for "wallhanger" flies. But even for fishing flies, this method cuts down on fluff in your fly box.

BUNGIE LEGS

If you tie a lot of bass bugs with rubber legs, an inexpensive source of the rubber legs is found inside the thread wrappings of a standard bungie cord. The rubber strands are of different sizes and come in various colors, too.

PRE-TAPE UNDERWRAP

This is a very thin foam, available at athletic stores. $3 will buy you at least a lifetime's supply. It takes dye well, it builds tapered bodies quickly and easily, and it smoothes out any irregularities before winding a tinsel body. Its uses are legion for a fly tyer

FALSE EYELASHES?

Fly tyers find uses for the darndest materials! False eyelashes make dandy tails on dry flies. The curve is just right and they tie in easily!

RECYCLING TEA BAGS

The stuff that is used to make tea bags also makes excellent winging material for dries. It won't disintegrate even in boiling water, readily accepts dyes and Pantone colors, and can easily be cut to shape. If you first use the tea bag for what its manufacturers intended, it will already have taken a dye bath, so, by adding a few veins with a Pantone or other permanent marker, you've got a very realistic component for your dry flies. Best to give the finished wing a coat of Flexament for added durability.

CHEESY FLIES

Don't overlook the possibilities of utilizing some of the modern packaging materials for fly tying. A case in point is the wrapping that Kraft uses for their cheeses. If it's not Mylar, it's Mylar's first cousin and, once cut into narrow strips with a sharp knife, can be used just like Mylar. I have before me a Copper Killer hairwing with a Kraft Cracker Barrel Baby Swiss wrapper body. Looks good. I have also used a strip of white material from a Frito Lay potato chip bag as an underwrap before using fluorescent floss; it seems to give the floss more "oomph."

WIRED FLIES

Copper wire cannot be faulted as a

component of flies - for ribbing, for adding a bit of weight, or even as tying thread as is the case with the Pheasant Tail Nymph. The most readily available source is ordinary lamp cord. I find it easy to handle if it is cut into lengths of 6 to 10 inches. Leave an inch or so of insulation on one end to keep the bundle together, and then just snip out a wire when needed.

SKINNY LEGS

The trouble with the commercial rubber leg material that is available is that it's too thick and not supple enough in the short lengths needed for small lures. The elastic sold in sewing and notion stores, made for waistbands in clothing, however, is perfect. The black stuff has really thin black lengths of rubber; the white can be left as is or colored with marking pens.

CUSTOMIZING WOOL

One evening while tying trout flies I was using Danville's Depth Ray fluorescent nylon and wool as body material. Although the color was exactly what I wanted, I found the material hard and ropelike to work with so I decided to try and customize it. I cut off a length of it, secured one end in the vise and with my fingers, carefully untwisted the two strands that made up the length of material. I slid my scissor points between the strands and ever so carefully separated them for their full length. I gently straightened out both pieces of material and placed them together again. The resulting length of material was smooth and soft, similar to dubbed wool, and lay on the hook shank just perfectly.

MORE TOOTHSOME GOODIES

Here's a new (new to me, anyway) product available at your local drug store called "Wide Space Dental Floss"

and what a boon it is to the fly tyer! It's a convenient length of dental floss covered with foam. The stuff is a dream to work with. It forms neat and well tapered bodies, perfect thoraxes on nymphs, and built-up heads for streamer flies. It can be dubbed over, or colored with permanent markers. Really a superb new addition to your materials collection.

CARPET FLIES

Almost any carpet supplier can provide you with an endless variety of left-over strands of carpet in a wide range of colors and textures. What a great source for wing material!

MORE FLOWER STUFF

A trip to the silk flower department of your local discount store can bring you a wealth of upright wings for dry flies. These flowers come in a wide variety of colors, some shaded from dark to light. They're easily trimmed to the shape desired, maintain that shape well, and are reasonably tear-resistant . The possibilities are endless and best of all, they're inexpensive.

MYLAR TAILS

Mylar drafting film makes excellent tails, especially for MOE saltwater flies. You can cut the tail in either a forked or narrow "V" shape as required to match baitfish or sandeel. Add a short stem that will be tied onto the shank or glued into the braided piping body. For added realism, the Mylar can be scribed with a black pen and coated with "Hard As Nails".

IMITATION BUSTARD

If you're having a tough time finding florican bustard for tying classic Atlantic salmon flies, try using goose shoulder which has been dyed tan, and make the wide black bars with a permanent black marker. When a slip of this feather has been married with the other fibers in a built wing, it's almost impossible to tell from the real thing.

THE HORSE, OF COURSE

I'm sure many fly fishers are familiar with the "Mite" series of flies, once tied with hair from a horse's mane. While clipping a bit of mane from a friend's horse I took a small bunch of tail hair as well. This latter has proven to be a most versatile material. I use a pair as the tails on Comparaduns; they make excellent substitutes on patterns calling for a monofilament rib; and nature provides them in many colors and diameters.

LIQUIDS

"To make black varnish for fly heads fuse 31 lb. of Egyptian asphaltum, and when liquid add 1/2 lb. of shellac and 1 gallon of turpentine. This varnish is a great improvement of ordinary spirit varnish. It lasts longer, and does not change colour in the water. "

George M. Kelson
Tips, 1901

HAZARDOUS SOLVENTS

Beware! Prolonged breathing of some solvents can be harmful. This is certainly true for some types of fly-tying cements, so when you use them make certain to provide adequate ventilation.

STICKY WAX

Those of you still seeking a really sticky thread wax should try a product used by cross-country skiers called "yellow klister." One popular brand, Swix, comes in a lead foil package about two inches high. Insert a bodkin into the package, then rub the bodkin up and down the tying thread for the length needed for dubbing. This product is especially good when making fur chenille bodies, since the fur can be applied at right angles to the thread with every confidence that it will stay right there until the dubbing loop is formed and twisted.

TACKY WAX

A good source of tacky wax for use in dubbing fur is the stuff used by paste-up editors and layout artists in their waxing machines for sticking paper and photographs to backing boards. The wax is available at any good graphics or art supply store—some brands are: Lectro-Stick Wax, PyraWax, and Artograph Wax. It is usually supplied in slabs that are scored into small squares that can easily be broken off. It's sold in boxes of five slabs which cost from $3 to $5. Since this is a couple of lifetime's supply, consider sharing a box with a couple of friends. It's stickier than the wax sold for fly tyers and is considerably less expensive.

DUBBING WAX

As every fly tyer knows, "tacky wax" is a great help when dubbing fly bodies with hard-to-manage materials. There are as many "secret" dubbing wax formulas as there are fly tying supply houses, each claiming theirs to be the best. Traditionally, the use of wax for dubbing purposes has remained unchanged over the years.

Matt Liquid Hairpiece Adhesive, made by Max Factor of Hollywood, California, made to keep a wig in place, is a wonderful, waterproof stuff with the right stickiness for dubbing. It couldn't be easier to use: just brush it onto the thread, stick on the dubbing, and roll it between your fingers. Only a trace of adhesive is needed.

It sells in a 3-ounce bottle, and comes with an applicator brush, which will last several seasons.

Beading it on the thread and

allowing it to set is recommended for hard-to-dub materials. This will squeeze surplus adhesive between the fibers making the dubbing material easier to manage. You can even paint a little Matt on your fingertips while rolling the dubbing. Matt has the same sticky qualities as adhesive tape, but is clear and thins with alcohol. A little dab on smooth-jaw hackle pliers helps to hold hackle feathers in place, too.

STREAMSIDE CADDIS COLORS
Latex-body patterns that match the free-living caddis larvae so well can now be matched by pre-tied flies in different sizes with natural-color latex bodies. Finish them with a short hare's-ear thorax with fibers picked out for the legs. If you carry Pantone markers in your portable fly-tying kit, when you get to the river and collect samples of natural, you can mark your imitations right there. You can match almost all caddis larva by carrying green, brown, tan and orange. It also cuts down on the numbers of flies you need to tie.

HEAD-CEMENT SUBSTITUTE
If you should happen to run out of head cement, a good substitute is clear nail polish. It's also available in white, red, and many other colors of interest to tyers. It dries quickly, is very hard, and works particularly well when it is necessary to build up a large head.

PLIOBOND SUBSTITUTE
Certain nymph patterns, such as Talleur's Perla Stonefly, call for feathers to be "preened" to shape with Pliobond cement. A cheaper and neater alternative is to use ordinary rubber cement, available at any stationery or art supply store. For preparing feathers it is used in the same way as the Pliobond, and gives the same results. As a bonus, rubber cement can be thinned as desired, is less toxic, doesn't smell as bad, and is much easier to remove from your fingers.

STICKY LIDS?
Avoid possible injury due to tapping a head cement bottle in order to loosen the lid.

A simple solution is to place a thin layer of Vaseline around the jar lid. Periodically you will find a renewed application to be beneficial. This makes opening the bottle much less frustrating and far safer.

EVER SPILL VARNISH?

To prevent spilling your bottle of lacquer or varnish, mount it in a bar of paraffin. Also, fill the bottle half full with epoxy, this reduces the volume. A cork with a needle adjusted just right will pick up the proper amount of varnish every time. Roughen the end of the needle with emery cloth so that it will hold the varnish. The bar of paraffin also makes a terrific place to hold your dubbing needle.

IMPROVED FLY FLOTATION
To improve the flotation of any dry fly, submerge the fly in Thompson's Water Seal for a minute or two—longer for large, heavily dressed patterns. Hang up to dry for 24 hours. Unscientific tests show that you'll be amazed at the longevity of the flotation, and the lack of discoloration of the materials. The inconvenience of the drying time is more

than made up by the excellent, high flotation of the treated fly.

HONEY, I SPILLED THE SUPER GLUE

If you find yourself with an unexpected need for a thinner for some CA glue you might try some ordinary fingernail polish remover. Most of these solvents will do the trick and can even save you from potential embarassment.

WAX CONTAINER

Having a problem with those too-large dubbing-wax containers?

Take a ChapStick container and twist the material all the way out and discard. Clear out the small cup and replace in the tube. Twist the cup all the way down to the bottom. Use a butane cigarette lighter to melt your original wax into the ChapStick container. When the wax cools, you can twist out the amount needed for waxing your thread. Replace the cap on the tube. All very tidy.

Paint the container a bright color and label it. Otherwise you might end up with sticky lips!

PREVENT EVAPORATION

Head cement dries up? Drop several marbles in the bottle. By raising the fluid level you reduce the volume of air, and this reduces evaporation of your solvent. It also makes it easier to reach the cement with your bodkin.

BLENDER STATIC

Some of the most effective fly patterns call for the blending of several colors or types of dubbing, be they natural furs or synthetics. Electric mini-blenders can cause fine furs like rabbit to cling to the sides and top of the blender container due to static electricity, a problem especially noticeable in the winter.

To all but eliminate this nuisance, wipe the inside of the blender container with a piece of clothes-dryer fabric-softener sheet. It doesn't even have to be a new sheet; one that has already seen duty in the dryer seems to work just fine.

MORE DURABLE FLIES

Zap-A-Gap is a cyanoacrylate adhesive (super glue) with gap-filling properties. Before attaching bead-chain eyes, put a tiny amount of adhesive on the hook, then lay on the bead chain. Wind the tying thread in the usual manner, and let the glue set for a few minutes. Result; the eyes stay lined up neatly on the top of the hook. When tying joints on salmon flies, most usually a flue of ostrich, a drop of Zap-A-Gap on the top of the body will hold both ends almost invisibly, and permanently in place. A fly such as the Colburn, with its center joint of ostrich, is made far more durable, and the wing will cover any mark that the adhesive may leave. Two words of caution, however; a little drop'll do you, and the stuff bonds fingers to fingers in seconds!

SPRAY ADHESIVE FOR QUILLS

Many times tyers like to coat a feather quill with cement to keep the fibers from separating. Take a Joe's Hopper for example. Strips of turkey tail are used for the wings. If the tail quill is coated with cement, tying in the wing strips is easier, the fly is neater, and more durable, and will not fray.

Applying head cement with a bodkin is a slow process. Spraying cement from a can is faster. Some spray adhesives are rubber based and very sticky when applied. This isn't what we want as the entire fly may end up all gummy. A good cement should be clear, water resistant, flexible, and fairly fast drying. It should not affect material color or alter any synthetics.

One spray has all these qualities. It is called Krylon Workable Fixatif. It is used by artists to prevent smudging of charcoal and pencil drawings. They spray it over the finished picture.

Simply spray it on any quill and let dry. Snip off the desired size piece and tie in a perfect wing.

Several brand names are available. Find it wherever drawing or artist supplies are sold.

HOT GLUE

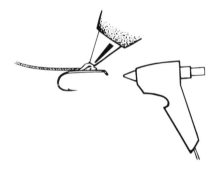

Some fly tyers are achieving interesting results with hot glue guns. By fitting a small diameter brass or plastic nozzle to the tip of the glue gun they are able to precisely place small drops of this adhesive where desired. Hot glue permits the instant fastening of lead wire parallel to the hook shank. It can be used to attach rubber legs, cork bodies, bead-chain eyes, and to bond slippery synthetics. It has even been used to form whole bodies for some saltwater flies. Use your imagination and experiment—you may find more applications.

PERFECT PENCIL POPPERS

One way to make pencil poppers or any other hard-bodied fly look especially nice is to give them a finish coat of epoxy. This helps to strengthen the body and protect the paint, and it looks great. By using an epoxy finish, you can use water-based acrylic paints. These are inexpensive, store well, are easy to use and clean up after, and dry fairly quickly, with no nasty fumes.

Older bugs that are beat up can be refurbished with fresh paint and epoxy, or just epoxy if the paint is in decent shape. You can even add a coat of epoxy to new, store-bought bugs so they'll look good longer.

Devcon 2-Ton seems to be the best brand of epoxy for this purpose. It dries clear, hard and smooth.

SUPER FLIES

For a fly that will never come apart some tyers use Super Glue, Crazy Glue or one of the similar CA glues in place of ordinary head cement. Try this and you'll never again have your thread unravel.

CONCENTRATED DYEING

Dyeing feathers has been reduced to a simple three-step process. Gone are the days of boiling pots, simmering pans, rubber gloves, chemical mixing and wives irate over the mess left behind. A Mason jar or large-mouth peanut butter jar, liquid fabric dye, vinegar and dishwashing liquid are all that are needed to complete the process.

The process calls for dyeing, transferring and drying. Pour the dye, vinegar and soap into the jar. Add the feathers and enough water to fill the jar. Tighten the lid and leave it overnight.

When transferring, use plastic salad tongs to pearl-dive for the feathers. After rinsing, lay the materials on sheets of newspaper in a flat place. The dye will keep and can be used for several seasons simply by shaking it up.

STORING HEAD CEMENT

Some tyers find it easiest to apply head cement with a small brush. Certain water-based type correction fluid bottles have just the right brush tip, are unbreakable and even have an insert that scrapes excess cement from the brush as it is drawn from the bottle. The neck is small enough to retard evaporation and it does not leak. It works great at home and in the travel kit. The only drawback is that it tips over easily if bumped by an errant hand at the tying table. This is solved by gluing a small, round ceramic magnet to the base of the bottle. Then cut a 2" round piece of thin sheet metal to place the bottle on. The magnet/sheet metal base won't tip if bumped

ROD-FINISH HEADS

When tying salt-water flies, many of which have long and/or large heads, Flex-Coat Rod Finish works as well as head cement. It's a great time-saver since one coat is all that's necessary to produce a beautiful, smooth head, and painted eyes are a cinch to put on. The one problem in using this finish is that it may sag or run unless you constantly turn the fly while it's setting up. Use a circle of Styrofoam stuck onto the shaft of a low RPM motor (such as a rod turning motor). The finished fly has a perfect, smooth head and looks great.

ENHANCING
FLUORESCENT FLOSS

To make the fluorescent butt on a salmon fly really shimmer and sparkle, try painting that area of the hook with typing correction fluid before winding the floss. ("White-Out" and "Liquid Paper" are two widely available brands.) The stuff dries almost instantly and for some reason, the white enhances the fluorescent quality of the floss even more than underwrapping with flat tinsel. Give this a try—you'll be pleasantly surprised at the result.

DYING LATEX

When using latex for shrimp shell backs only a limited number of colors are available. At the Tandy chain of crafts stores you'll find a large color selection of permanent dyes intended for use on leather. They work equally well on latex.

COLORED LACQUER HEADS

Applying colored head lacquer directly to newly-tied heads has two drawbacks. First, pigmented lacquer is too thick to penetrate the thread wraps for maximum strength. Also, if any lacquer touches adjacent materials, it is often "wicked-up" by those materials resulting in pigment spreading into unwanted places.

To avoid these problems on flies that require colored head cement, make an initial coating with clear, high-penetrating cement. You'll end up with a stronger and neater result.

MICROWAVE DYEING

You can dye grizzly feathers in a microwave oven by placing a natural grizzly hackle feather between two feathers that have been previously dyed to the color wanted for the grizzly. For example, to dye the grizzly red, place the natural grizzley between two red feathers, then wet the feathers and place them in a plate with a few drops of water in it. Next place the plate into a microwave oven and zap it for three minutes. When the feathers are done "cooking" remove them from the microwave and separate them. The result is an evenly dyed grizzly hackle that has taken on the color of the two outside feathers.

COOKING UP COLORS

Using your microwave oven for the dying of fur and feathers has several advantages over conventional stove-top techniques—assuming of course that it does not result in any significant domestic confrontation. By using a temperature probe you can precisely control your dye bath temperature, most commonly maintained at 190 degrees. Also you can place small quantities of dyes in glass containers which both saves on dye and provides for much easier clean-up.

ONION-SKIN DYE

To get a "lemon" shade of mallard flank to substitute for the scarce and expensive lemon woodduck flank, try boiling a handful or two of dry onion skins. Strain the liquid into another container holding washed mallard flank feathers. Stir, and leave the feathers in the liquid until they are tinted the proper shade. Drain, place the dyed feathers in a pillow case or other smaller, cotton bag, and tumble dry in a drier. It's a close match to the real thing.

HOME COLORING

While many tyers don't want to get involved in dying their own materials, there is one process which can be handled rather easily at the bathroom or kitchen sink. That is the bleaching or coloring of furs, hair and feathers using products designed for use on human hair. You can easily lighten or darken your materials in order to obtain that elusive color you've been seeking. Simply follow the instructions on the package, but remember—it's better to begin with a diluted solution, especially when working with feathers.

HAIR CONDITIONER

If you wash bucktails, calf tails, and other hairs before using them (a good idea in itself) the hair will be prettier and easier to work with if you also apply some hair conditioner. Use whatever brand you have, or buy the cheapest—it doesn't matter.

Hair conditioner also works on hackles. Wash the cape, rinse, then apply the conditioner according to the label instructions. After blotting off excess moisture use a blow dryer on the feathers. The results are amazing.

COFFEE DYE

A coffee dyebath is one method used to obtain the perfect shade materials for a Light Cahill. First completely clean and thoroughly rinse the material to be dyed, usually a white/cream neck, white rabbit fur, and gray mallard-flank feathers. Bring two cups of water to a boil, add four heaping tablespoons of instant coffee and two teaspoons of acetic acid. Add your materials to the solution, let simmer for 10 to 15 minutes. Remove from the heat and let steep for another 15 minutes or more. Remove the materials and rinse in cold water.

THINNING CEMENT

When diluting head cement, pouring thinner can be messy, especially when it runs down the side of the bottle onto your tying bench. You can eliminate the mess by drilling a hole in the lid of an empty head cement or thinner bottle and place an eye dropper, available at most pharmacies, with a big enough squeeze top to pull it through the hole, holding it in place. An eye dropper with a measurement scale makes it easy to control the amount of thinner you add to the cement. The eye dropper always stays in the lid, making it easy to add thinner to head cement, spill free.

SAVE YOUR SPRAY

The idea of spraying dry flies with Scotch Guard at home to lengthen the life of your fly flotant on the stream is not new. The problem, however, is that the spray broadcasts too large an area, the fumes are not healthy, and the Scotch Guard is wasted.

A solution is to spray the Scotch Guard into a glass jar (a baby food jar is ideal). On contact with the jar it becomes "liquid" Scotch Guard. Simply dip your finished fly into the solution and set it out to dry. Close the glass jar lid to save your excess solution!

This solves the problem of mess, fumes, waste and extends the life of your dry fly flotant on the stream.

BETTER BOTTLE TOPS

Replace the screw-on lids of lacquer and head cement bottles with corks of the proper sizes—they're available at most pharmacies. Insert toothpicks into the undersides of the corks. These stoppers are easier and quicker to remove than screw-on lids, and the toothpicks make the application and amount of lacquer applied far more precise than using a brush.

SMALL DYE LOTS

If you have to dye up a bunch of #10 hackle for a batch of green drakes, why dye the entire neck or even a half. Remove the #10 hackles you need, strip the fluff from the butts and bind together with tying thread. It will be easier to dye now because you won't have to put up with the greasy chicken skin in your dye bath. In addition, when you need the #10 hackles, you won't have to hunt for them on the neck, they will all be in a small neat bundle. Also, it requires less dye and a smaller container to work in.

PRESERVATION

To preserve old gut on snelled flies, add one ounce of glycerine and one-quarter teaspoonful of baking soda to four ounces of distilled water. When not displaying the flies, it is best to keep the snells wrapped in a cloth saturated in this mixture, and with plastic wrapped over the cloth in order to prevent evaporation.

MORE STATIC

A product, sold in Canada by Alberto-Culver, called "Static Guard" solves annoying static problems when tying with deer hair or elk hair. Spray the hair and tying tools to stop the static electricity that makes the hair stick to everything. Use of the Static Guard also makes the stacking and clipping of animal hair neater and easier. This product also stops the fly-away tendency of Flashabou.

A LITTLE DAB'LL DO YA

Dubbing wax is great stuff for helping to hold dubbing to thread but using more than just a little bit is very apt to discolor the fur. Try stroking the wax onto the thread and then rubbing your fingers up and down the thread to distribute just a light coating of wax. Your dubbing will hold just as well and the discoloration of your carefully blended dubbing will be minimized.

NO-PEST STRIPS

If your fly tying setup is a permanent one, try hanging a couple of "no-pest strips" overhead to control any insects that might be in the area. Another idea is to remove the waxy strip inside the cardboard case of the "No-Pest strip" and cut it into small (about 1" square) pieces and put one or two in each of your materials containers, be they boxes, drawers or plastic bags. This method is all but guaranteed to rid your stuff of such destructive insects as hide beetles which, if left alone, will quickly demolish incredible quantities of fur. A word of warning—the chemical contained in the waxy strip which you have just cut into small pieces is not healthy, so be sure to wash your hands thoroughly after handling.

TIRED OF UPSETTING THE HEAD CEMENT?

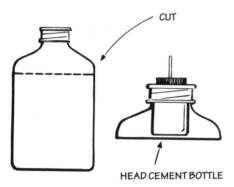

HEAD CEMENT BOTTLE

You can eliminate head cement spills by cutting off the top of a fairly large-mouthed plastic bottle and putting the head cement bottle inside it. The wide base makes spills a thing of the past.

MORE ON MOTH REPELLENTS

If the smell of moth balls (naphthalene) really gets to you there are other products that will perform as well and smell better while doing their job of protecting your valuable fly tying materials. Blocks or boxes made of cedar wood are a definite improvement in aroma and while not as inexpensive as moth flakes, are very long lasting, needing only a touch of sandpaper to expose more of the fragrance. They are available in closet shops and through some mail order catalogs. Drug stores have or can order cake camphor, which is made of the oil extracted from camphor wood and will also do a fine job protecting your fur and feathers.

MORE STATIC

I seem to pick up a lot of static electricity—not uncommon in dry climates. This often creates a problem when tying with elk and deer hair. Nothing is more frustrating than to sit down to tie and find that you are a magnet. Every bunch of hair you touch leaves half of itself stuck all over your hands. Here's an easy and permanent solution, however. Computer supply houses sell grounding strips which attach to a computer keyboard and are grounded to an electrical outlet. They cost less than ten bucks and are a cinch to install. Simply touch it with your fingers before you begin to tie and all the static electricity you are carrying will be gone.

CA WITHOUT WASTE

Cyanoacrylate glue, or Super Glue, or CA cement, has become a standard furnishing on most tyers' desks. Here's how to avoid plugged up containers of the stuff. Build a wooden fixture to hold the container in an upright position. Make it from scrap wood, either round or square, just so that the bottle can't fall over and spill. That's the answer. Don't put any kind of a cover on the container—no pins, no wire, no caps, no pieces of Teflon rod—nothing. It won't harden, evaporate or lose its strength. Mine has been on my bench, open, for eleven months and it's still unplugged and still full strength.

BEAUTY SHOP GOODIES

The small bottles of model paints that are used to paint cork-bodied popping bugs and heads of large streamer flies are a real pain. Once opened, they are difficult to seal up, resulting in thickened or dried out paint. Besides, the brushes have to be cleaned after use. We've all used "Hard As Nails" or a similar product as a head cement substitute. Comes in a neat little bottle with a brush in the lid, all ready for use, and no clean-up afterwards. Carry this train of thought further. Does any manufacturer make anything besides red, pink and clear nail polish? You bet your boots they do! Any color you can think of is available: black, white, orange, purple, green, blue, and don't overlook the glitter finishes either (suspensions of metal flakes in a clear polish base). And all these products come in neat little bottles with brushes in their lids! For use in finishing fly heads, the brushes work better if they are trimmed slightly in both length and girth. The larger drug and variety stores usually carry the offbeat nail colors, or if all else fails, try a beauticians' supply store, and disregard the raised eyebrows and strange looks you'll get. These products will cost you around a buck a bottle, and they're worth every penny!

NAIL POLISH WITH TEETH

Nail polish is useful for more than putting a glossy finish on the heads of your flies. There's a new (to me) product on the market sold under names such as "Matte Finish Base Coat," "Nail Mender with Fibers," and so on, which consists of a clear or opaque nail polish containing thousands of finely chopped plastic or fiberglass fibers. These tiny fibers point every which way and so the liquid has, in effect, a matrix to harden around. The original purpose was to provide a strengthening base coat for fingernails and to provide a slightly rough surface for the color coats to adhere to. These products also make superb tying cements. Paint a thin coat on the hook shank before winding chenille or wool and the finished fly is nearly indestructible. If you have trouble with coarse dubbing, a layer of one of these base coats on the shank will help to lock in the shaggy fur. It's sticky, dries fairly quickly, is easy to

apply as there's a brush in the cap, and it is relatively inexpensive.

GET A HANDLE ON DYING

Cut opening

The handiest dye receptacle may be the simple one gallon milk jug. The drawing tells it all—cut out a hole larger than your hand on the side away from the handle. Dump in the dye, half fill the jug with the hottest tap water and mix well. Insert through the hole previously washed materials, still damp, stir thoroughly, and about 15 minutes later, fix the solution with a slug of vinegar. If a deep color is desired, just let the material soak in the dye solution overnight. Grab the jug by the handle to empty the dye, and rinse the dyed material, still in the jug, under the tap, and then dry on a bed of newspapers. No mess at all.

ENVIRONMENTALLY RESPONSIBLE ACCELERANT

A number of patterns call for the use of cyanoacrylate glue in their construction, and the use of a spray accelerant for the glue. These accelerants may contain freon, which is not environmentally friendly and can harm the ozone layer. Instead, use baking soda. It makes a great accelerant and will help neutralize the odor of the glue.

Just sprinkle some on the part to be glued and blow off the excess. This will leave a thin film, just enough to accelerate the glue. The other alternative is just to allow the glue to set on its own - it really doesn't take that long.

SPRUCING UP YOUR EPOXY

Tubes of printing ink, available at most hobby shops, come in many colors and do not cost much. By putting a tiny amount into the epoxy when you mix it, perfectly colored heads result. You can also cut up some Mylar tubing into the epoxy to give it extra flash.

GOOP HEADS

To make durable and realistic heads on bass and saltwater flies, try Shoe Goop. Tie up the fly and leave it in the vise. Squeeze the tube from the bottom and force out a ball of Goop and transfer it to the head of the fly. Moisten your fingers so the Goop doesn't stick to you and form and shape the head of the fly. If you want to add eyes just press them into the still-wet Goop. When the fly dries, you'll find that the head is light and translucent, permitting the colors of the materials beneath to come through.

RECYCLING NAIL POLISH BOTTLES

Used fingernail polish bottles make wonderful containers for fly cement. The problem is, how to fill them as they have such very narrow necks. After you've thoroughly cleaned out the bottle, and dried it (a hand-held hair dryer works well for this chore) hold the bottle over the can or bottle of material that you want to fill it with and dip a screwdriver into the material. Remove the screwdriver and hold it over the neck of the nail polish bottle and let the varnish, or whatever, drip into the neck of the bottle. It takes a few minutes, but results in NO MESS, always a popular move at my house.

A LITTLE DAB WON'T DO YA!

The other day at my local fly-tying shop I was reminded that things that seem obvious to those of us who have tied for a while, are anything but to newer tyers. A fellow approached me and asked how I got such lovely shiny smooth heads on my salmon flies. "Head cement," I answered. "What kind?" he asked. I mentioned the name of a common brand. "Gee, that's the kind I use, but the heads on my flies always look rough" he said. I enquired the number of coats he was applying and I saw a light go on. "I've been putting on one coat, as much as the head would hold, but the results leaves a lot to be desired. Maybe I should use two coats?" I laughed and said that the very minimum number of coats I used was four, and often more layers than that, leaving plenty of drying time between each. He went off muttering to himself, but I'll bet the heads on his flies look a lot better from now on.

NEW GLUE?

A new cement used by the construction industry is called "Liquid Nails." Widely available in caulking gun form and less so in a tube, it is used for putting up panelling, including Styrofoam. It's one of the very few adhesives that does not dissolve Styrofoam. It is rather like thin chewing gum in consistency, but it sets up quickly and is very sticky. Works great for gluing on eyes, as well as making thin streamer bodies from sheet Mylar—fold a piece of mylar over the hook shank, apply a bit of Liquid Nails to one side, and then squeeze the two sides together. When the adhesive dries, cut the body to shape.

DEER BODY HAIR

"Above all, fly-tying is immensely enjoyable as a creative activity, conferring aesthetic bliss upon even minimal manual skill. Great satisfaction is to be had simply by storing up materials, preparing dye baths, dubbing fur, clipping deer hair, folding wing cases, winding hackle, and performing all the pleasant little tasks associated with this most engaging pastime. Perhaps tying flies is the closest any of us get to playing God."

Robert Boyle & Dave Whitlock
The Fly-Tyer's Almanac, 1975

TOUGH THREAD

If you break the tying thread when spinning deer hair, start using dental floss to construct bass bugs. The Butler shred-resistant unwaxed dental floss is enormously strong, yet will not cut the hair when you snug it down. Available only in white, the floss can easily be dyed by using a Pantone marker. It can be purchased in a number of different-size containers, from 15 to 300 yards. The 100 yard spool is perfect as it will fit into a bobbin like any other spool. It has one other quality that is hard to resist. It's cheap!

EASIER TRIMMING

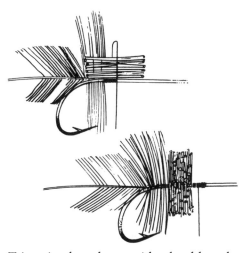

Trimming bass bugs with a hackle collar can be a difficult task when you're trying not to cut any hackle fibers. Tying down the collar works fine but requires an extra tying step. Here's a shortcut that eliminates the extra step.

Cut the first bunch of deer hair short enough so it won't need any trimming after it is tied on to the hook. The trick to this procedure is to keep the tips of hair even at all times. The rest of the bug should be completed in the usual way, and trimmed.

MUDDLER HEADS

When tying in the deer-hair collar on a Muddler Minnow, do not cut off the butt ends of the deer hair. Add red dubbing onto your thread and wrap it directly over the thread winds securing the deer hair. Push the butts back with a half-hitch tool (ball-point pen without its refill), then tie in the rest of the deer-hair head and clip the head. The purpose of this red dubbing is to separate the collar from the head so the collar does not get cut off in error. This is particularly useful on smaller size hooks such as 10 and 12.

TRIMMING MUDDLER HEADS

After the deer-hair head is spun on the hook, take a section of plastic drinking straw, 1/2 to 3/4 inches long, and slice it lengthwise. Then slip the straw over the head of the fly, back to where the deer hair ends form the collar. By turning the straw as you trim the head of the fly, none of the collar hair is cut off, and a neat muddler head results.

TRIMMING DEER-HAIR BUGS

One of the problems in tying deer-hair bass flies arises during the hair trimming process, especially on those bugs with a splayed hackle tail and hackle collar. How do you trim the hair without cutting the hackles?

After tying the tail, and wrapping the hackle, pull the collar backward toward the tail, and, while holding it tightly, wrap 4 or 5 turns of .025 lead wire around it securing it in place. The lead keeps the hackle out of harm's way as you trim the deer hair, and is easily removed once you've finished all trimming.

DEER HAIR STRIPS

If you tie a lot of flies using natural deer body hair here's an idea which might be of interest. Take large pieces of deer hide and cut them into long, thin strips which might range from 1/4 to 1/2 inch wide and 5 to 10 inches long. The length should be cut "with the grain" and the cut is best made from the back of the hide. This is most easily accomplished if you are working with a tanned hide. The resulting strip provides a highly convenient source for consistent-size bunches of deer body hair.

SHAPING HAIR BODIES

Many tyers have trouble making smooth, even bodies and heads on flies made with deer-body hair. You trim, it's uneven. Retrim and end up with a mutant with its large body and small head.

Remington has recently marketed a battery-powered razor for nose and ear hair called the "Sanitary Razor." The head of the razor is small enough, (1/4"), to trim almost any size fly. After rough trimming the fly with scissors, Use the razor for the final trimming. Works great.

I've been told that the Groomsman II, beard trimming razor works great, too.

EASY HUMPIES

Humpies, or Goofus Bugs, are not the easiest of flies to construct but here's a tip that may help. After tying in the tail fibers, Scotch tape them to the vise. Then, when collecting the deer hair to form the "hump", there's no need to separate the tail hair from the body hair. When the fly is finished, carefully remove the tape. This procedure has saved endless aggravation.

SPINNING DEER HAIR

Most "how to" books on fly tying say not to wind thread on the shank of a hook before you spin deer or other hollow hair around it. These books caution that if there is anything between the hair and the hook shank, the hair will not spin properly. Not so. Wrap size A rod-winding thread on the shank as a base, and not only does the hair spin perfectly, but when you pack each clump of hair back, you can actually feel the tying thread lock into the notches between the thread wraps covering the hook shank. This method results in a denser and more durable fly.

BUOYANT DEER HAIR

Deer hair flies float well due to the hollow hair used in their construction, but in time they will become waterlogged. Try this. In a wide-mouthed jar standing in a pan of boiling water melt two parts paraffin with one part of mineral oil. Mix well. While the mixture is hot, dip the bass bugs, mice, bombers, etc., and stir them around until saturated. Remove and squeeze out as much of the mixture as possible. If necessary, stroke the hair back to the correct shape. A hair lure so treated won't become waterlogged, and one sharp back cast will free it of water.

BURNING EYES

When burning the eye sockets into spun and packed deer body hair with a heated finish nail, it is really a pain to carry the alcohol lamp used to heat the nail. Try using a wood burner. The handiest tool uses the 3/16" blank round tip.

The tip is perfect for four to six millimeter eyes. Larger eye sockets can be formed by burning out the edges around the 3/16" tip eye socket.

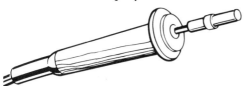

Steps for burning eye sockets:
1. Allow the Hot Tool to preheat.
2. Lightly mark the eye position with the burner.
3. Burn the socket to the desired depth and size.
4. Use tip of dubbing needle to remove burned portion.
5. Place a drop of cement in eye socket. (Use Goop, Epoxy, or 527 Cement)
6. Place eye in socket and adjust while cement is drying.
7. Remember, skin burns at the same temperature as wool and deer hair!

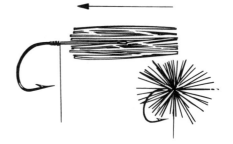

When tying bass bugs, muddlers or other patterns calling for clipped deer hair, here's a simpler method of accomplishing this than the conventional technique of laying the deer hair on the hook shank and tying it so that it first rotates around the shank and then flares. Take a pencil-sized clump of hair and slide it over the eye of the hook so that the hair lays parallel to, and surrounds the shank completely. Then a turn or two of thread around the hair to hold it, another couple of turns using more tension to flare it. The result is even coverage of hair on all sides of the shank, and later, when you trim and shape the hair, there will be no bare spots.

PREPARING SPUN DEER HAIR
FOR TRIMMING

Trimming muddler heads and shaping deer hair bugs is a problem for some of us. Whether you use scissors or a razor, the hair has a tendency to slide away from the cutting tool, and the result is often a "chewed-on" appearance. Try steaming the deer hair before you make the final trim. Tie the fly as usual, and rough-shape the hair with scissors. Remove the fly from the vise, and grip it in hackle pliers or tweezers, and steam it. The hot steam swells the cut hair and shrinks the tying thread which packs it more tightly on the hook. Finish the shaping with a sharp razor blade. You'll be amazed at how easily the hair can be trimmed.

BASS-BUG RAZOR

With this razor you can shave your bass bugs, Dahlberg Divers, mice, or any other hair bug. Using a handle from an X-acto carving set, insert a Schick injector razor blade into the handle's slotted collet. The blade will fit perfectly. You will now be able to barber your bass bugs like a professional. When the protruding end of the blade becomes dull, just reverse it and use the other end. This not only works better than holding a blade between your fingers, but it's a lot less likely that you'll cut yourself. If you want to trim in a tight area, grind the back of the blade to a width of about 1/8 inch to the shape shown.

THE FINISHING TOUCH

A twin-bladed razor is an excellent tool for putting the finishing touches on your deer hair work. These shavers remove very little hair so it's nearly impossible to ruin a bass bug with a single cut. Use these razors to smooth out the "tool marks" often left by trimming deer hair with scissors, for shaving the belly of a bug perfectly flat or very close to the hook shank, or for scooping out hollow spots where doll's eyes will be glued. A nice extra feature of these tools is that you can't slip and slice open a finger or two.

SCORCHING SPUN DEER HAIR

When tying spun deer-hair bodies and heads like sculpins or bass bugs, try scorching the finished, clipped hair with a match or lighter. This flares and seals the hair making heads and bodies waterproof.

SPLIT SHOT SPINNING

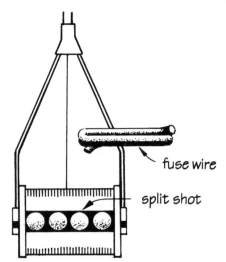

fuse wire

split shot

When spinning deer hair for bass bugs, etc., try putting fuse wire or three or four #5 split shot in the hole of the thread spool. The shot is held in place by the bobbin's feet so it won't fall out. The weight of the bobbin will prevent any loosening before you get the next clump of hair spun. It does away with taking a half hitch after each bunch of hair and speeds up construction.

COMB YOUR HAIR

When spinning hair it's essential that all the underfur be removed to allow the individual hair fibers to flare evenly. Most of the swatches of hide will have some underfur which will have to be taken out before the fur is fit for use. A mascara comb/brush, found at any cosmetic counter works perfectly. The comb side is about as wide as the largest bundle of hair you can spin, and the teeth are long enough to go through it. Just cut the hair off the hide, and while holding it firmly by the tip ends, place it on your tabletop and slowly comb out the underfur and fuzz. You'll also get rid of most of the shorter hairs, giving you a clean bundle of hair to work with. The brush side of this tool is handy to rough up nymph bodies.

DUBBING

"Fly-tying is breaking loose from some of the tighter fetters of tradition. Tradition is a hallowed part of fly-tying, but tying would not grow in innovation or appeal if we adhered to the practices of ancient Macedonians or fifteenth-century English nuns or even to the dicta of the sainted Theodore Gordon."

Robert Boyle & Dave Whitlock
The Second Fly-Tyers Almanac, 1978

ADDING LIFE TO DUBBED-FUR BODIES

Any fly tyer who has ever used hare's ear or mask has to admit that the small amount of difficulty encountered in using the dubbing is outweighed by its fish catching properties.

To add liveliness and translucence to the natural fur dubbing, the next time you are mixing up your furs, strip the herl off 2 or 3 peacock quills and mix it into the fur.

You will find it adds just enough to your flies—not to make them gaudy, but more like the natural you wish to imitate.

DUBBING TROUBLES

As a technique, dubbing goes back a long way in the history of fly tying. Judging from the literature, our predecessors had as much trouble as we do, and usually for the same reasons. Probably the most common problem, which is that of the dubbing not staying on the thread can be solved by one or both of the following tips: first, use a lot less fur and apply it in layers, winding back and forth if a thick body is needed. This technique makes for a very durable fly body. Tip two is to twist the dubbing onto the thread in *one direction only!* Absolutely, positively DO NOT twist the dubbing onto the thread with a back and forth motion of your fingers. For a right-handed tyer twisting the "noodle" of dubbing onto the thread with a twisting motion toward the head of the fly seems to work best.

INDUSTRIAL-STRENGTH DUBBED BODIES

There seem to be two ways to dub bodies. One is to apply the dubbing material to a single waxed thread and by pressing and twisting it between two fingers, adhere the dubbing to the thread. The other method is to make a dubbing loop, hold the loop open, spread out the material within the loop, and then spin it, forming a chenille. Combine the two methods for extra durability. First wax the single thread, and apply the dubbing. Then make the loop, spin it, and wrap the material onto the hook shank, forming a very tightly dubbed and durable body.

TESTING FOR COLOR CHANGES

Take a small amount of dubbing, mixed to the exact color of the body of the natural fly, wet it and hold it up to the light. Frequently it will be several shades darker than when dry, and in some cases, it will assume an entirely different color than that of the natural fly.

WIRE-CORE DUBBING

Using fine copper wire instead of thread, for preparing looped dubbing "noodles" has several advantages. The wire adds both strength and weight; even a bit of flash and color if desired. Make up a quantity of colors and take them with you to streamside. They won't untwist and can be used to change colors of your bodies. The flexible copper wire secures easily to any fly.

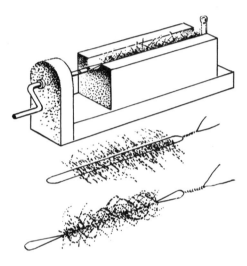

To prepare wire core dubbing make a dubbing twister as illustrated, and collect an assortment of colored wire from old electrical parts.

SPIKY DUBBING

Tie your nymph, scud and even wet-fly patterns with spiky dubbing. The result is more takes by selective trout. Unfortunately, much of the dubbing material on the market today, whether natural fur or synthetic, is just not spiky enough. Try this—clip the hackle fibers from the feather of a cape or saddle and add these fibers to the dubbing. Softer hackle fibers add a soft spike to the dubbing and tend to fold back against the fly body in the water. Stiffer fibers stand out from the body and pulsate more actively, especially in faster water. Pull

the feather from the cape or neck, run your fingers along the stem to separate and straighten the fibers, and scissor them into the pile of dubbing. Mix well, and build the fly body using the dubbing loop method. An added benefit is the ease with which the color and stiffness may be varied.

INSTANT & EXPERT DUBBING

One of the most difficult procedures for a beginner to master is the fine art of dubbing. A UHU Glue Stick, available at stationery stores at a cost between 75¢ and $1.50, depending on size, can be used as a dubbing wax. Make a pass with the glue stick down the tying thread, and using your usual dubbing technique, apply the dubbing material. You'll find that it's lots easier to work with than dubbing wax, and your fly bodies will be much better looking.

NO-WAX DUBBING

Instead of using wax on your thread when dubbing bodies, use a dab of hand lotion, spreading it evenly on the thread with your fingers. I find it quicker and easier than wax.

DUBBING THE EASY WAY

Most tyers have all kinds of trouble arranging dubbing evenly in a dubbing loop. Here's a real easy way - just leave the fur on the skin until it's in the loop! From the skin side, cut a narrow strip of fur. Place the fur in the dubbing loop and then cut the hide away from the fur. Spin the loop as usual and wrap the fly body.

CLEAN DUBBING

When tying dubbed dry fly bodies it's always been difficult to make certain that there are no long guard hairs in the dubbing. By accident one day I found the solution. Dub the thread, using a single length and then, just before you start winding the body, tighten the tension on the thread and pluck it as if you were plucking a guitar string. This causes the guard hairs to stand out, away from the thread and then it's easy to pick them out. And prior to tying a wet fly or nymph, you can use the same trick to achieve a "buggier" looking fly.

IMPROVED "DUBBING THE EASY WAY"

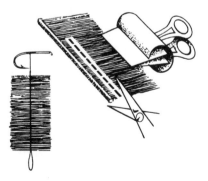

Purchase two 3 or 4 inch binder clamps at any stationery store. Cut the fur strip

or hair in whatever width you want and place the hide end into the jaws of one clamp and then pull the hide out tight against the inside of the jaws. This insures even lengths of fur. Then attach the second clamp over the hair extending out from the first clamp. Remove the first clamp, then cut the hide from the fur. Place the fur into the dubbing loop and spin. The amount of fur is easy to vary, as is the length of the fur or hair. Works like magic!

SECURE DUBBING

If you untwist your tying thread before you apply fine dubbing, and then retwist the thread, the fine fibers will be locked into the thread and hold the dubbing very securely.

LOOP METHOD ASSISTANT

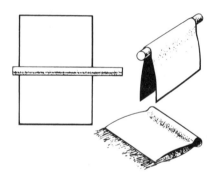

From .003 brass shim stock, I made a handy tool to help me when I use the loop method for dubbing. Take a piece of brass about 1" X 1 1/2" and fold it in half over a 1/8" dia. wire; then make a second one. With this pair of tools you can trim an aftershaft or fur to be dubbed to any width you want. I put the dubbing on my knee in the density that I want and pick it up by sliding the bottom leaf of the tool under the fur or feather, then pinch the leaves together and place the captured material into the dubbing loop in one motion instead of a bit at a time.

WATER BLENDING FURS

If you don't have access to an electric fur and dubbing blender, here's an old-timer's trick that works just as well. Fill a canning or jelly jar half full of water, put in the material to be blended, replace the top, and shake like crazy. Drain into a strainer and allow the blended dubbing to dry between paper towels or newspapers.

SAVING BITS OF DUBBING

A piece of felt or furry foam works quite well to hold small leftover quantities of dubbing. And try a larger piece of either material when a small quantity but large selection of dubbings will be needed, for example when you're travelling. Just place a small amount of all the various colors that you think you'll want on the fabric and then roll it up.

DUBBING MIXER

Try a battery-powered clothes shaver to mix dubbing as well as to cut overly coarse dubbing into finer bits.

EYES & LEGS

"... the fly angler's success is certainly more satisfying ... with artificial flies. ... If he ties his own flies, he becomes every bit as creative as the person who paints pictures from nature, and, even better, he discovers a new dimension to fly angling."

S. R. Slaymaker II
Tie a Fly, Catch a Trout, 1976

GUITAR-STRING EYES

To make perfect, round black eyes for nymphs and other flies, instead of using monofilament, stop by your local music store and ask for "Ernie Ball" black nylon classical guitar strings, sizes 1 and 3. The #1 string is for smaller eyes, the #3 for larger ones. The stuff melts in a flash to a perfect round ball, and ties-in very easily.

KNOTTING LEGS

Many tyers experience difficulty when tying a knot in goose biots. In order to do this task without going insane, use a tool that is probably on your workbench right now—a bobbin threader. This tool is easy to make: simply bend an eight inch length of fine steel leader into a long, slim, diamond shape as illustrated. Tape original ends together to form a handle.

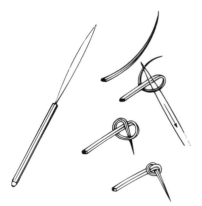

Make a small open loop with the biot, reach through the loop with the bobbin threader and snare the biot's tip, then pull it back through the loop.

The "leg joint" can then be positioned and tightened with ease.

LEGS IN FOAM

Until you've tried to insert rubber legs through foam flies, you won't know what a pain it is. This method makes it easy, though. Ask your veterinarian to give you a large syringe needle. Thread the rubber leg through the needle and insert it through the foam body of the fly. Grab the rubber leg on the far side of the foam body and withdraw the needle. Trim the legs to length, and the job is done. When you're finished, be sure to replace the plastic cover over the needle—them things is sharp!

CREEPY-CRAWLY LEGS

Bass bugs look so much "buggier" with rubber legs protruding from their sides. The attachment of these legs has always proved to be a hassle. Knotting, tying figures-of-eight, or gluing, made the spinning of the remaining deer hair difficult, not to mention the problem of keeping the legs in position.

Complete the bug and trim to shape. Using a large-eyed darning needle (available in most needle assortments) thread one end of the rubber leg through the eye. "Sew" the leg through the tightly packed deer hair on top of the hook shank. Pulling down, while holding both ends of the leg, will lock it in place. The leg can be cut to the desired length, or repositioned, by judicious pulls. This is a quick and effective method for adding life to a bass fly.

SEWN LEGS

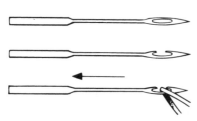

This will save your fingers when sewing leg material through foam bodies. First, beg, steal or borrow a sewing-machine needle. Place it in a vise and remove a part of the eye as illustrated. Insert the needle into a pin vise which can be purchased at any hobby shop, then push the needle through the foam body, place the leg material into the notch, and pull back through. This is much easier than using a regular needle.

STRIKE UP THE BAND

Rubber legs add a tremendous amount of action to bass bugs, and the movement attracts prowling bass. No need to shop the catalogs to find these pieces of rubber—plain stationery store rubber bands will do just fine. Buy them as large in circumference as possible (the curved ends are not much good for bug legs) and either knot them around the hook shank as you tie, or thread them through the finished bug with a needle. You'll find you catch more fish on leggy bugs!

SPARKLING EYES

By now most fishermen agree that adding eyes to flies, poppers and bugs adds to their productivity. Make eyes for your flies by using a hole punch on Prismatic tape. This produces a neat round eye, and a small dot of Testor's black paint in the center of each eye makes the pupil. Then just peel the backing paper off the eye and apply. To insure that the eyes stay stuck, coat them with head lacquer or Flexament. To attach these eyes to feathers, first coat the area with cement to make sure they are firmly attached, and then coat over with clear cement.

CHEAP RUBBER LEGS

Rubber legs, as many tyers have discovered, are an effective addition to bass bugs, panfish flies, and stonefly nymphs such as the Bitch Creek.

A lifetime supply of rubber legs may be as near as the trunk of your car or your garage—elastic "bungee cords."

These cords are composed of hundreds of thin rubber strands—just the right size for legs! The braided cloth covering can be cut open with a razor blade to reveal enough rubber legs for a thousand bass bugs.

EYE EYE

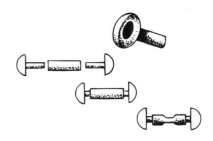

Securing stemmed plastic eyes to the head of a fly is not easy—if you tie them side to side, one is further back than the other. Gluing the tips of the stems together is not strong enough. Here is a method which utilizes the steel sleeves used for making leaders. Insert the stem of each eye into the sleeve, fastening it with epoxy. Do the same at the other end of the sleeve, then crimp it in the middle. This crimp permits the eyes to sit low on the hook shank, and once tied on securely, they tend to stay in place. This system is great for saltwater Puffs, hair bugs and dragon flies.

MONO-BENDING

Here's a way to make shaped monofilament legs for your flies without having to worry about tying knots for the leg joints. With this process, you can make very attractive legs.

To make the Mono-Bender just take a 3/16" to 1/4" wooden dowel, a fine diameter sewing needle, and some type of heat resistant epoxy. Push the eye of the needle into the end of the dowel and apply the epoxy. You can use your bodkin, but on small diameter legs it's usually too bulky.

Before attempting Mono-Bending on your finished flies, you might want to first practice. Heat up the Mono-Bender with a candle for a few seconds. Immediately wipe off the black soot on the needle, then hold it next to a monofilament line. You'll see the line bend toward the needle. You can bend the line as much as you want or wherever you want. Warning: Do not touch the heated needle to the monofilament. It will melt it instantly.

After you've practiced, tie up some flies with monofilament hanging straight out. Wait until your fly is completely finished before you form the legs.

PIN BEAD EYES

Most notion counters, sewing stores and some hobby shops carry boxes or papers of stainless steel pins which have round glass heads instead of the usual flat metal ones. These pins make excellent eyes for bass bugs, prawn flies and some nymph patterns as well. Just make certain that the shanks are stainless steel and not nickel plated. Cut off most of the the shank leaving enough length to bend into a hook shape so the eye can't pull out, and tie in at the head of your fly. If you're feeling adventurous, try some of the other colors as well!

BEAD EYES

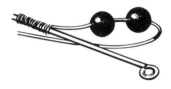

John Betts, master of synthetic materials, introduced a novel idea by using ordinary round black beads to represent eyes on his small streamer patterns. He first attaches one end of a piece of thin monofilament on top of the hook shank, leaving the free end pointing forward. Next two beads are threaded onto the mono which is now folded backward and secured to the hook shank. Positioning the beads with figure 8 wraps is all that remains to provide you with simple, effective and attractive eyes for your flies.

EYED FEATHERS

"Slick Pens" made by Tulip Productions Division of Polymetrics, Waltham, MA 02254, are used for painting on fabric. The paint, when dry, is waterproof, and at about $3.00 for a set, they're perfect for painting eyes on streamers or spots on the wings of such patterns as Lew Oatman's Brook Trout streamer. It takes a bit of practice to get the spots just where you want them, but the results are very satisfactory.

LEAD EYES

These weighted eyes were designed to sink crab and shrimp imitations, for both bonefish and permit.

Equipment to assemble your own lead eyes includes: rosin-core solder, a soldering iron or gun, flux, tweezers, thin bladed knife or single edged razor blade, and copper wire in various sizes.

Select the diameter of solder that will result in desired weight. Lay some solder on a firm surface and slice off small doughnut-like sections. Select copper wire with a diameter equal to, or smaller than, the hole size in the solder. Cut wire to the desired length, and place it into the hole in the solder, holding it as shown so the wire protrudes 1/2mm to 1mm.

Heat the soldering gun, put a small amount of flux on wire, touch hot tip of gun to spare solder to pick up a small quantity on the tip, momentarily touch tip to end of wire, and remove gun as soon as solder drops forming a half-round ball.

Repeat this procedure to form the second eye. This is much easier to do than to describe. Try it, it's simple and fast.

PAINTING LEAD EYES

One of the best leech patterns uses painted lead eyes. The problem is holding them as they are painted—you get more paint on your fingers than on the eye.

By using a woman's bobby pin you can hold the middle of the eye in one of the wavy notches of the pin. It does not matter if the middle of the lead eye gets painted or not because that's the part that gets tied on the hook. If you remove the protective coatings on the opening end of the bobby pin, you can stick that end easily into a block or styrofoam cup so the lead eyes can dry.

EYE GUNK

Many fly fishermen advocate the use of eyes on certain patterns. The type of plastic eye with a moveable pupil encased in a clear plastic bubble seems to be particularly realistic, and they're available in a variety of sizes. The only problem is attaching them securely to the fly. Here's what works well.

When hot glue guns first appeared on the market, they were clumsy and difficult to control. The molten adhesive seemed to have a mind of its own, continuing to issue from the tip of the gun long after pressure had ceased. But all that has changed and the current models permit great precision.

The type of glue marked "All-Purpose" or "Craft and Hobby" is fine for our purposes. Apply a small dot of glue to the head of the fly and gently press the eye in place. Glue one side at a time. Although you will have to work rather quickly there is adequate time to position the plastic eye before the glue sets. The strength of the bond is amazing—on a scale of 1 to 10, it's somewhere about 11, whether the head of the fly is thread or clipped deer hair. The inherent flexibility of the glue seems to insure the eye's survival even after the roughest treatment.

One note of caution—the tip of the gun gets quite hot (380 ° F.), but the glue itself has none of the health hazards associated with solvent-based adhesives.

PAINTING EYES

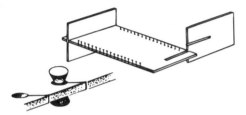

If you've ever tried to paint lead eyes holding them in your fingers or with tweezers, you know how impossible a task it is. However, about 20 minutes of time will enable you to build a rack that will simplify this chore tremendously. You'll need some scrap cardboard—matboard from a framing shop works well—a drill, and sharp knife or razor blade (or bandsaw, if you have one).

Three pieces of matboard are cut as depicted. The slits in the two smaller pieces will fit at right angles into the slits in the ends of the longer piece, and allow the rack to be safely handled and turned to either side when you're painting the eyes. Slits in the longer piece of cardboard can be cut with a sharp knife or razor blade, although a more convenient method involves drilling holes at the bottom of the slits with an electric drill prior to cutting the slits with a bandsaw.

DOTTING EYES

Most stationery stores carry a typewriter eraser that looks like a pencil but which has a brush on one end. Buy one, cut off the brush and sharpen both ends. Then cut back one end until you get the size circle you want for the eye. Cut back the other end until you get a smaller circle for the pupil. Dip the end with the larger circle in the colored lacquer and apply to each side of the fly head and let dry. Then dip the smaller circle in contrasting lacquer and apply in the center of the larger circle to indicate the pupil. Be certain to wipe the lacquer off the eraser after each use.

STICKY EYES

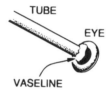

Many streamer, bucktail and bass bug patterns call for dolls' eyes to be attached to the head of the fly. These can be hard to hold in place, and I've tried many cements and glues with varying degrees of success. I've finally settled on a glue gun and a simple way to hold the eye in place while the glue sets. The glue requires only seconds of pressure to set, and to hold the eye in place while that's taking place, Use a short length of plastic tubing, one end of which has been dipped into a jar of Vaseline. Press the tubing onto the top of the eye, press the eye into the glue and hold the eye in place until the glue sets, and that's that. Just wipe the Vaseline off the eye and it's done.

BUG EYES

Santa brought my daughter "Puff Paints;" the kids use them for painting their own designs on shirts, shoes, sofas, etc. They are easy to apply, come in small applicator bottles, are no-mix,non-toxic, machine washable, and available in a rainbow of colors, including neons and glitters. They're available in craft and fabric shops. The potential is limited only by your imagination.

To paint eyes, either directly onto the trimmed hair or in recesses burned in, first apply the iris color—white, yellow or whatever—and before that color tacks up, apply a dot of color for the pupil. If you apply directly on trimmed hair the result is a wonderfully bug-eyed and froggy look. These eyes are lots easier than epoxy— no mixing, no dean-up, and they won't fall out like dolls' eyes.

DOTTING EYES

Everyone has a pet tool for every tying operation and perhaps we get a degree of satisfaction out of hand-hewing our own implements, and, if there is nothing like it available, that's the way to go. There's no need to make a tool for painting perfect dots of varying diameters, because the drill-bit index manufacturers have done the work for us. With a standard drill index you're set to do single dots or multi-ringed eyes on any size fly head or lead eye.

EYES BY THE YARD

If you've been searching for a product that is easy to use, cheap, and doesn't involve melting monofilament to provide eyes of various sizes for a variety of patterns - mice, crayfish, nymphs, etc. - search no more. At a fabric and sewing supply store you can find a product called "Pearls by the Yard." They come in a continuous chain, in a bunch of colors and diameters, take paint well, and best of all, cost less than a dollar for a yard of them. Each length will make a lot of eyes on your flies!

WASTE NOT, WANT NOT

When mixing epoxy, it seems as if there's always a bit left over. Rather than waste it, make the eyes that can be used on streamers and bugs. The simplest way to make these eyes is to tie a knot in the end of a piece of monofilament and dip the knot into the epoxy. Dry it in the rotisserie, or on a slow-rotation motor used to dry rod windings. When dry, you can paint the eye(s) and then re-dip in the next batch of left over epoxy. The size of the eye is controlled by the size of the monofilament and the number of times you dip it.

EASY LEGS

Here's a trick which you can use successfully on nymph and hopper legs. Heat a sharp-pointed pair of tweezers and squeeze the hackle legs to the angle you want. Release the tweezers and the result is a perfectly formed leg angle. A bit of experimentation is needed here - too much heat and the hackle breaks; too little, and the bend does not hold.

SPECKLED RUBBER LEGS

I use natural cream-color rubber hackle for my stonefly nymph legs, but before I tie them onto the fly, I mottle them with various Pantone pens. I double over a strand of rubber and clip both ends in hackle pliers, then hook the middle of the loop over a nail and pull on the pliers to straighten the strand and color it with olive, several shades of brown and a bit of black. Don't coat the whole strand, but let a bit of the natural color show. The result is a leg that looks much more natural than the uncolored rubber, and it has the added advantage of good durability.

REALLY SPARKLING EYES

When making saltwater "Siliclones,"

instead of using decals for the eyes, buy a package of sequins at the sewing store. They are packaged in multi-color assortments so that you always have a choice of colors, and they *really* sparkle.

DO-IT-YOURSELF LEAD EYES

You'll need a pair of long-nosed pliers with wire cutters, a pair of flush-cut pliers, and a roll of solid lead wire solder about .125 in diameter. With these three items you will be able to make hundreds of lead eyes for your flies and lures. First, grind a groove into the wire-cutting part of the long-nosed pliers. The opening should be large enough that it will notch the solder, not cut through it. Use a 1/8" stone in a Dremel tool to accomplish this, closing the jaws on the stone so that both sides of the cutter are ground evenly. Then cut a 1/2" piece of solder, center it in the notch you've ground, and close the pliers. There. You have a pair of lead eyes that need only to have the ends trimmed to the length that you want. A bit of paint, and they're ready to be attached to your fly. A $3.00 roll of solder will provide you with enough material for a lifetime of tying.

HERLS, STEMS & QUILLS

"We cannot take a brush and color our patterns as we would like them to be. But we can use more intelligence in our choice of materials. . . . Assuming reasonably skilful tying, our flies stand on whether or not we employ proper materials in the proper way."

John Atherton
The Fly and the Fish, 1951

BRONZE PEACOCK HERL

Some fly patterns specify that the peacock herl used for the body should have a bronze tone rather than the more common metallic green color. This hue can be achieved by placing a peacock tail feather in direct sunlight for a several weeks, where it will gradually bleach to the desired color.

TOUGH QUILLS

The problem with using sections of duck, turkey, goose or similar quills is their lack of durability. A trout's teeth will cut the quill to ribbons, especially when they are fastened at both ends as in nymph wing cases. A solution to this problem, if you can call having a trout's teeth cut up one of your flies a problem, is to take a small embroidery hoop and tightly stretch a piece of ladies' nylon stocking over it. Using a flexible bonding material—Pliobond or Flexament are possibilities—cement the quill segment to the nylon, and let it dry. You have a section of quill that is as tough as the nylon to which it is bonded. Now if we can only do something about the tougher problem of getting the trout's teeth onto the fly . . .

GLUING HERL

Here's a trick for affixing peacock herl to the hook shank that really holds the herl in place. First wrap the hook shank with tying thread. Tie in herl, then lightly coat the thread wraps with Flexament or head cement. Wind the herl and tie off. The slightly tacky cement will hold the herl tight to the hook shank and prevent its unwinding, even though broken by hard use. Take care not to put too heavy a coat of cement on the hook—just enough to stick the herl stem to the thread-covered hook shank.

TOUGH BUTTS

If the fly being dressed calls for an ostrich or peacock herl butt, try using fine chenille instead. Chenille is available in all colors and it is a far more durable material than herl. Tie the chenille in under the hook shank, make one full turn of the material, which is usually enough, and tie off under the hook shank.

BURLY HERL

Peacock herl didn't get to be one of the most ubiquitous of fly tying materials because it doesn't attract fish. As a body material, it's unbeatable. The individual fibers move enticingly in the water; light brings out its magical and ever-changing color—blue, green, copper and gold. Only one thing wrong with it—it's fragile. About the easiest way to overcome this drawback is to tie in a length of either dark colored thread or fine wire before you attach the herl. Then wind the herl body, tie off, and counter-wind the body with the thread or wire. The thread or wire being wound in the opposite direction to the herl will serve to keep the herl tight to the hook, and the result is a more durable fly.

EQUAL QUILL-WING SECTIONS

There are many types of dividers or wing-formers used to insure equal sized wing segments, but what works best for me is a pair of scissors. Working from the back of the feather, separate the fibers with the points of your scissors. Place the points where that separation meets the shaft of the feather. Lightly draw the scissor points down the fibers, next to the quill. Each time you pass over a fiber you will feel a slight "bump". Measure the size section you need by counting those bumps. Cut the section free and repeat on the opposite wing feather. If you count the same number of fiber bumps before cutting, the sections will be equal.

HOW TO STRIP

Peacock quills that is.

Fly tyers have discovered a number of effective techniques to remove the flue (barbules) from the quill (actually a barb) of a peacock tail feather —take your choice. The first requirement is to select the proper quill from an eyed peacock-tail feather. When tying quill-bodied flies the best results are obtained by choosing a quill from either side of the shaft at, or immediately below the eye. The available methods are:

1. Lay the quill on a hard surface, press your middle finger on one end and your thumb on the other end. Using an ordinary eraser simply rub off the short fibers (flue).

2. Place the butt end of the quill between your thumb and index finger of one hand, pressing against the quill with the thumbnail. Grasp the butt end of the quill with your other hand and pull the entire length of the quill under pressure—but not so tight as to break it. Repeat this process until all the flue is removed, usually two to four times.

3. Dip the entire peacock eye into melted paraffin—let cool. Once the wax is hard select an individual quill. When you break away the wax the flue is removed with it.

4. Place the quill on a hard surface and scrape it lengthwise with a knife or single-edge razor blade.

5. Immerse the entire eye into a bowl of Clorox for one or two minutes until the flues detach, and then immediately rinse in a solution of baking soda and water to neutralize the bleach. Rinse and dry. Some tyers store these quills in a small ziplock bag with a few drops of glycerine and water.

6. Spray the eye with a clear adhesive spray such as Grumbacher's Tuffilm. Let dry and peel off with your thumbnail—the flue will come off too.

MAKING HERL CHENILLE

If you wind your tying thread around the peacock herl a few times and then wind them on the hook together, the thread will prevent the herl from breaking the first time a fish attacks the fly. For a fly that will see heavy use (salmon, steelhead or very large trout), make a dubbing loop and then twist the herl in the loop.

QUILL SOFTENING

One of the best body materials for dry flies is quill. Used on such wonderfully productive patterns as the Quill Gordon and Red Quill, it imitates the segmented body of many insects without adding any weight or bulk to the fly. It does present one problem though. Many quills are brittle. This drawback can be overcome however. In a small, screw-top jar mix a solution of one half to one third glycerine (available at any drug store) and the balance tap water. Once you've removed the barbs (or herl) from the quills, place the quills in the glycerine and water solution, and leave them there. Stiff quills should soak a minimum of 24 hours before use; the best part is that they can remain in the solution indefinitely without any ill effects. When you're ready to tie a quill-bodied fly, remove a quill from the jar, quickly squeegee it between your fingers, tie it in, wind it, and tie off. This had best be done quickly as the solution tends to dry quickly once removed from the jar, and the quill will soon become brittle again. Once the body is wound and tied off, put on a couple of coats of head cement to protect the fragile material from trout teeth.

ANOTHER STICKY TIP

Here's another terrific method for securing both dubbing and herl. Thin Pliobond cement and apply to thread, place the dubbing on the thread, form loop, and twist. Use the same technique with peacock herl, except don't form a loop.

STRENGTHENING PEACOCK HERL

Reinforcing peacock herl is always a problem. Sure, you can overwrap with thread, or twist thread around it, but here's a method that not only strengthens but also adds a bit of sparkle. Use a strand of blue-green Crystal Flash and twist it around the herl before wrapping the fly body.

BIOTS

Biots, a.k.a. stripped goose quills, are the long tapered barbules found on the leading edge of primary wing feathers. They're used mostly for tailing nymphs. They are not however, unique to goose quills—in fact, they are found on almost any primary wing feather—duck, pheasant, whatever. For example, you can find long tapered, beautifully mottled biots on pheasant quills; some are perfect for midge sized flies. So be

sure to check quills from any birds that come your way. There are some great biots out there.

PRE-PAIRING WINGS

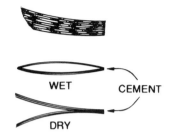

This tip not only speeds up tying but also makes winging wet flies a lot easier as the feather slips can't get out of alignment. Cut slips from a left and a right feather and place them together and align as though you were about to tie them in. Cut off the butt ends evenly, apply a dot of head cement in between the butts and hold for a few seconds to allow the cement to set. Then lay the pre-paired wings aside to dry. Do a couple of dozen pairs at a time - one size - one color.

BRAIDED HERL

Here's one more way to increase the durability of peacock herl bodies - braid three strands together before wrapping around the hook shank. It only takes seconds, and it does make a nice body on those patterns.

SPLIT-FREE QUILLS

When stripping quills, the bleach method tends to dry out the quills which then become very brittle while in dry storage. To cure this, you can rub a small amount of cooking oil or baby oil on the quills before storing them. The oil softens the quill so that it winds around the hook shank beautifully, no matter how long ago you actually stripped the quill.

QUICK-SNIP QUILL WINGS

When tying with matched quills, duck, turkey or the like, carefully line up each quill and tape them together top and bottom. With this method you only need to pick up one item, and if the feathers are properly paired up, both wing slips can be snipped off at the same time.

DENTAL—FLOSS QUILL

Unwaxed dental floss, when soaked in tea, coffee, or iodine can be used to replace stripped peacock quill. It's a lot tougher and more durable, and costs next to nothing.

WEIGHTY MATTERS

"There may be as many schools of fly-dressing as it takes nails to fasten a horseshoe. I do not know. It is, however, certain that all of them are right in the river for which they were designed and will kill fish better than the ordinary type which lacks some quality with which the local tie has been invested."

Eric Taverner
Fly Tying for Trout, 1939

WEIGHTING A LEADER

Weighting a leader is simple, effective and durable, and puts a fly right on the bottom. Besides your leader you'll need some Pliobond, methyl ethyl ketone—MEK (available at auto paint shops) and some powdered lead, available at golf-club shops that specialize in customizing or repairing golf clubs. Immerse the leader, either knotted or knotless, in hot, soapy water for about five minutes and rinse. Hang the leader from any place high enough to accommodate an 8' leader, and weight the tippet end. Use a small drill vise with the jaws padded with rags or inner tube. In a small tin can, thin the Pliobond with a small amount of MEK, and add some of the powdered lead. Use a popsicle stick to mix. When the stuff takes on the consistency of thick cream, paint it onto the leader, using a small paint brush. Be careful not to let it build up over knots. Paint it on to all except about the last eight inches at the tippet end of the leader. Let dry overnight. Be sure to take adequate precautions when mixing and applying—well away from open flames, pilot lights, etc., in a well-ventilated area, and wear rubber gloves. Mix only what you think you'll use as the mixture cannot be stored.

Now for the blessings of a leaded leader. The fly will get to the bottom of a big fast river in record time. There's no sinker to get hung up. It's a miniature shooting head. It's incredibly strong. Best of all, it lasts for years.

FOILED AGAIN

The lead foil found on most corked wine bottles provides a free source of weight for nymphs, streamers, and even for leaders. When opening the bottle of wine, carefully slice off the top portion directly over the cork; then make a vertical slit down the neck of the bottle and remove the rest of the wrap. After flattening it, you'll end up with a 1 1/2" x 4" sheet of lead foil, the thickness of which will vary from bottle to bottle. These sheets can be cut into strips using a razor and steel edged ruler or by using two utility knife blades separated by a plastic or metal shim of the appropriate thickness. Both 1/16" or 3/32" seem to be good all-around widths. The strips will wind around a hook shank almost like flat tinsel and cause little or no bulge in the body of a finished fly. And acquiring this material can also be enjoyable.

SINKING GLO-BUGS

Single Glo-bug flies have a tendency to float, particularly in the smaller sizes, and wrapping the shank with lead wire does not allow the yarn to flare properly. But taking heavy lead wire and flattening it with a hammer or in a bench vise to a very thin sheet, wrapping it around the hook shank and securing it with Kevlar tying thread before attaching the yarn seems to work well. Although the bug will not sink like a stone, this method does, remove a good deal of unwanted buoyancy.

WEIGHTED THREAD SPOOLS

Between steps of tying a fly you want the thread to remain taut. To do this weight your bobbin by filling the spool's center hole with cut-to-length pieces of lead wire. Once the spool hole is filled, remove the bundle, wrap with thread, and seal with head cement. The solid lead cylinder may be easily transferred to any spool.

MARK YOUR WEIGHTED NYMPHS

It's easy to remember which nymphs are weighted when you're looking over a batch freshly tied, but it's another tale months later when you're staring into the contents of a well-used, mixed-up and often-tangled fly box at streamside.

A favorite way to prevent such confusion is to use a different color thread for the heads of all weighted flies—or at least a band of colored thread (or wire). Some tyers even differentiate between lightly weighted and heavily weighted flies by using a three-color system.

WEIGHTING GAME

Rosin-core solder makes a good material for weighting flies. It comes in a variety of sizes and is available at hardware and Radio Shack stores. It winds easily, and can be melted and molded with a soldering iron to become a permanent part of the hook.

FLATTENING LEAD

Most beginning fly tyers have trouble making a tapered body when using lead wire to weight the fly. A simple method is to use the non-serrated section of the jaws of needle nosed pliers to flatten the wire before you wind the body. By varying the pressure used you can vary the thickness of the wire—thinner where you start to wind and at the head, thicker for the center of the body or thorax. Make sure that the turns of flattened wire closely abut each other but do not overlap.

PART TWO

In order to flatten lead wire to eliminate bulk when tying small flies, try using the wooden roller that is customarily used for laying Formica. By varying the pressure you use, the thickness of the lead can be controlled. It is best to wind an underlayer of thread on the hook shank before wrapping the lead as the thread will help hold the lead in place.

THE BEST LEAD WIRE

The lead center from a lead-core fishing line is one of the best materials for weighting flies, for the simple reason that the dacron covering has imparted a texture to the lead. By underwrapping the hook shank with tying thread, then placing the lead strips along the shank and binding tightly with thread, the textured lead provides "teeth" that grip tenaciously—no twisting of the nymph body. This textured lead also provides a fine medium for shaping and sculpting underbodies.

Removing the woven covering of the lead requires only that you run your thumb and forefinger along the section of line until it is straight, push down the covering at one end for a quarter inch or so, and, holding the covering just below where your fingers are holding the lead, pull gently. If you hold the covering at the end away from the uncovered lead, you'll be creating a Chinese finger puzzle, and the covering will never slide off.

ZONKER UNDERBODIES

Pull-tabs from aluminum cans have frequently been recommended as the underbody for Zonkers. However, the lead tape available from golf pro shops is easier to use and more satisfactory. This tape is customarily wrapped around golf-club shafts to add weight. It's sold in half-inch wide rolls with a peel-off plastic backing, and is often sold in lengths from a large roll.

The tape can be cut to the desired length and folded along the center before the backing is removed. The backing is then peeled off and the tape positioned on the hook shank. The lead can then be trimmed to the desired shape and size.

SLIP-FREE LEAD

When tying lead wire onto a hook, most tyers discover that the stuff tends to roll, slip, pile up, and look less than neat. The usual cure is to wrap on lots of tying thread in an effort to fix or at least disguise the problem. There is a better way.

Wrap a thread base on the shank of the hook as usual. Tie in the wire parallel to the top of the shank, then lift it to enable you to spiral the thread forward. Then wind the lead tightly around the hook shank as usual, stopping with the lead pointing straight up. Bend the wire sharply 90 ° to the right and parallel to the top of the hook

shank. Tie the end down and cut off the excess. Flatten both ends of wire so that they form a smooth transition with the shank. This method secures the lead firmly, and provides a neat base on which to tie the fly body.

WEIGHTY CHAIN

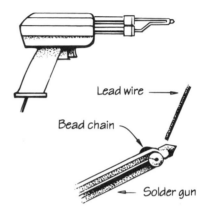

If you want to add even more weight to flies that will be tied with bead chain eyes, try placing the pair of beads into the soldering iron as shown in the drawing. Turn the iron on and feed lead wire into the holes in the bead chain. The heat from the iron will melt the lead wire and fill each bead.

LEAD PACKING
You can compress the lead wraps on your weighted flies by using a deer hair packing tool. This can result in more weight on the fly and/or provide you with more space for other materials.

IMPROVING PATTERNS

"... no fly is the 'ultimate,' no pattern will always catch fish and I for one hope that no such fly will ever be designed. The main attraction that fly-fishing holds for me is in its constant testing of my small skill at selecting the fly which is correct for that particular moment and in which the fish will show an interest; mostly I am wrong but as the years pass I slowly learn from my mistakes."

David Collyer
Fly-Dressing, 1975

GLOW-IN-THE-DARK FLY

Following the example of lures that phosphoresce for salmonids and bass, here's how to create a glow-in-the-dark fly. Find a plastic rope that kids use to make bracelets, lanyards, etc., that is slightly larger in diameter than a fly line and is available in 18" lengths. It works nicely as a substitute for the pearl mylar tubing used in so many streamer patterns. Cut a piece of glow rope to fit the hook shank, attach to the underside of the hook, and finish the fly. This rope is available in two colors, green and hot pink. This fly has been especially effective just before dark, and when the water is muddy. Some fishermen are using an inexpensive camera flash to "charge" the fly for night fishing.

SERVE UP SOME
BREAD-AND-BUTTER NYMPHS

Two of the most successful and most popular nymph patterns are the Gold-Ribbed Hare's Ear and the Casual Dress. Both of these flies have proved themselves by accounting for thousands of trout and other fish.

Broaden your nymph selection by tying each of these in colors different from just the natural brown rabbit or muskrat gray. Your variety can be further increased by producing them in a wide range of hook sizes. For light colors begin with bleached fur which can be dyed light olive, and such. Dark colors don't require the bleached fur.

You can easily fill a fly box with colored Hare's Ear Nymphs alone—and you'll be prepared for lots of fish. And even fill another box with weighted ones!

SINGLE WING MAYFLIES

Most dry-fly patterns for adult mayfly imitations specify that you tie upright, divided wings. While this style of wing is in the finest tradition of our sport, many modern anglers would admit that there may be no advantage to the double wing compared to a single upright wing. In fact, most mayfly duns hold their wings together upon emergence. You can simplify your tying by using the single wing style for your mayfly imitations and the fish won't know the difference.

FAST WATER-SLOW WATER

When tying imitative patterns in preparation for the upcoming season, think about where these flies will be used. A caddisfly, for example, is often tied full and bushy for fast-water conditions so it will float high and can be seen in turbulent water. Slow-water conditions, on the other hand, dictate that the same caddisfly be imitated with a sparser, more realistic dressing. It's often a good idea to prepare some of each style when you get your materials out.

SEE IN THE DARK

Do you have trouble seeing your fly during late-evening hatches? Often we find ourselves fishing in virtual darkness. One suggestion is to add a small amount of fluorescent material to the wings of my patterns. One such material is sold as "EverGlow" and probably is available under several other names. Just mix three to five pieces of this material into the winging material and tie in as usual. Sometimes it is necessary to recharge the Flashabou with a flashlight. Glowing wings may not make a traditional looking fly but the trout don't seem to mind, and your eyes will be grateful.

FLASHBACK NYMPHS

Try using a strip of wide silver Mylar tinsel for the wingcase of your mayfly nymphs. It adds flash and seems to imitate the tiny gas bubbles produced by the natural insect.

SAN JUAN WORM

In some tailwater fisheries one of the more popular flies is the San Juan Worm, a representation of a naturally occurring aquatic worm. To achieve the realistic tapered appearance of a worm try attaching a length of Vernille (sometimes called Ultra-chenille) to the hook

leaving both ends extending out. How to taper the worm? Easy. Burn each end! Practice a few times on scrap pieces until you see just how much heat and for how long. (It doesn't take much, and don't use direct flame) Rub the burnt ends between your fingers to remove the charred part and voilà, a tapered worm!

RIBBING STREAMERS

To get more flash from tinsel bodies, some streamer patterns call for oval tinsel ribbing. When using Mylar tinsel, here's the same effect with another technique.

Start at the eye of the hook and wind to the barb end with closely abutting turns of thread. Then wrap back to the eye of the hook spacing the wraps to about 1/16" or even further apart if you are tying on a large long-shanked hook. (On these large hooks you can use monofilament to make even more of a protuberance.) Then wrap your tinsel tightly from front to rear and back again and tie off. Two coats of Hard as Nails and the body is finished.

FINE RIBBING FOR SMALL FLIES

It's difficult to improve on a pattern like the Troth elk-hair caddis. But one suggestion is to replace the fine wire ribbing with tippet material, in sizes 5X to 8X, especially for flies size 16 and smaller. The wire tends to break at the point where it's tied in at the tail. There seems to be no change in the appearance or performance of the flies tied with tippet ribbing. You can also use this material to counterwrap the body and palmered hackle on Griffith's Gnats.

FISHAIR GRIZZLY

Tyers of saltwater flies can use Fishair barred with a permanent Magic Marker as a replacement for the more fragile grizzly saddle hackles called for in many patterns. Break off a small (not more that 1/2"wide) piece of Fishair from the bundle and run a comb through the hair to get out the tangles. Spread out the hair and clip the bottoms to a piece of cardboard. While stretching out the hair with your left hand, mark a stripe or bar on the hair by making a series of adjacent dots across the Fishair with a marking pen. Repeat until you have barred the entire length of Fishair, then flip it over and repeat on the other side. A fine-tip marker will allow you to make thin bars and place them very close together, but except for small flies this is not really necessary. The variety of colors available in both permanent marking pens and Fishair can keep you experimenting for years, but do yourself a favor and try black bars on white, lime green or royal blue Fishair!

START WITH WHITE

Some materials, particularly light-color synthetics used as body materials, become somewhat translucent when they get wet, either from water or from dry-fly flotant. This results in a color shift as the dark hook shows through, changing the intended appearance of the fly. You can control this by first painting the hook shank with a coat of white paint or lacquer. Let dry, then tie your fly. The colors of the materials will remain true, even when wet. There appears to an increase in translucency as well.

HEADLIGHT MUDDLER

By mixing a 50/50 blend of Crystal Hair and deer-body hair you are able to create a very sparkly effect when applied in the customary way as with the deer hair alone. Use this to create a version of the muddler minnow called the Headlight Muddler, which has caught fish when nothing else worked.

BODY BY CRYSTAL HAIR

Crystal Hair, a synthetic material recently introduced to fly tyers, consists of very thin strands of translucent material connecting tiny globules of the same material. It is a very interesting and versatile material.

For tying Trico duns, try wrapping a single strand of pearl-colored Crystal Hair over an olive thread body. The effect is incredible; the finished fly is almost iridescent. Experimentation with different colored threads and various shades of Crystal Hair will produce a match for the Tricos in your locale.

The easiest way to wrap Crystal Hair around the size 24 hook was to use hackle pliers. And Crystal Hair must be carefully tied off or it can slip loose.

Experimenting with Crystal Hair as a ribbing material in lieu of wire or thread. Crystal Hair certainly makes flies look more lifelike.

CURE FOR SHORT STRIKES

All fly fishermen have experienced the frustration of having fish strike short. Changing patterns, changing hook sizes—nothing will induce a fish to stay stuck. Here's what my fishing partner and I have come up with, and it works more times than not.

Tie a sort of tandem fly - with the trailer hook much, much smaller than the front one—and no further back than the tail of the fly. On size 12, 14 and 16 flies use a size 20 trailer; on size 18s and 20s use a size 24 or 26 hook. It does not seem to impair the castability or floatability of the fly and it sure helps hook the short strikers. Just don't forget that it's there when applying floatant or sinking compound—those tiny hooks hurt like the very devil when buried in a finger.

TOUGH TINSEL

After winding a tinsel body on a fly, try overwrapping it with monofilament, Swannundaze or V-rib. The tinsel will not only be protected from from tearing, but by using a colored overwrap the tinsel will assume its tint. The body of the fly will be somewhat larger in diameter, but the flash of the tinsel through the plastic wrap is a real tantalizer for trout.

SPARKLING FLIES

The use of crystal or sparkle chenille gives a whole new dimension to fly bodies. On nymphs, woolly buggers, leeches, and similar patterns wrap an underbody of the stuff, leaving a small gap between turns before winding the body dubbing and see how much more life the patterns have. The amount of flash can be controlled by the texture and thickness of the fur dubbing.

MUDDLER HEADS WITHOUT TEARS

There seems to be a point in the tying of most flies at which a pretty one turns into an ugly monster. For me, that point was reached when trying to tie deer hair heads on Muddlers. It was time-consuming and the results were unpredictable. I bought a few pieces of "Craft Fur" at the local craft supply store, in colors that seemed useful. I cut off about a 1 inch clump of tan and put it into the blender, and following Grandmas recipe of "a pinch of this, a little of that," I added a little brown, a dash of yellow, a bit of clear Antron for sparkle, and blended them all together. Then I finger-blended some of the resulting

mix into a bundle slightly less than the diameter of a pencil, and tied it in at the head of the Muddler. A bit of work with the little brush that came with my electric razor and that I never use anyway, or an old toothbrush, to fluff up the ball of dubbing, then some quick scissor work, and there's the Muddler shape head, all finished!

COLORFUL STREAMER WINGS FROM HEAD TO TAIL

When tying bucktail streamers with multi-colored wings, try using "Invisible Thread," which is nothing more than fine monofilament and is available at sewing stores. Tying the head of the fly with this transparent thread lets the wing colors continue right up to the eye of the hook, instead of being interrupted by the usual black thread head.

HERL SUBSTITUTE

If you like to tie nymphs with peacock wing cases, try substituting peacock colored Krystal Flash. It's a lot more durable and adds a bit of flash to the fly.

MEATY NYMPHS

Prince nymphs, Zug-bugs and other herl bodied nymphs can be given a new look by winding a strand of ostrich herl over the peacock; black ostrich will give the nymph a darker look; light ostrich a lighter look; and best of all, the extra flue on the ostrich results in more motion in the water and a meatier looking nymph.

FISH-LIKE SCALES

Many tyers have difficulty in creating realistic looking "scales" on their streamers. Here's an easy way to accomplish this. After you wrap the hook shank with either gold or silver mylar, overwrap with closely butting turns of monofilament, 20 to 40 pound weight, depending on the size of the hook. Not only does this create an amazingly life-like "scaly" look, it also increases the durability of the fly enormously.

LIGHT YOUR DRY FLIES

If you fish much in the late evening or at dark you know how difficult it can be to locate your dry fly. One solution which is claimed to be effective is to tie your flies with slightly oversize white calftail wings and then coat the wings with glow-in-the-dark fabric paint which can be purchased in most craft shops. The paint is waterproof so it doesn't wash off easily. At streamside just shine your flashlight on the luminous paint and you can get 5 to 10 minutes of hi-visibility fishing before another recharge is necessary. If you become addicted to this idea you can even carry a small, battery charged camera flash attachment for more intense recharging.

TRICKS & TECHNIQUES

"As long as there were fur and feathers and colored thread, there were hope and possibility and excitement—the chance of success."

Harry Middleton
The Earth is Enough, 1989

CLIPBOARD STRIP

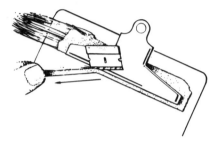

Having trouble cutting even strips of rabbit skin, chamois or Ultrasuede for Zonkers, mouse tails, etc? Try using a clipboard. Place the material that you want to cut into the jaws of the clip. Using a razor blade, Olfa blade or similar tool, cut along the face of the clip. Move the material the width of the strip that you want, and cut again. Leave from 1/4" to 1/2" at the top of the cut to keep the strips attached to the skin until you're ready to use them. Suede and chamois can be cut tight against the board, but rabbit skins must be skin side up and pulled up off the board while cutting so you don't damage or trim off the hair.

TIE MORE SIZES

The most common mistake made by beginning fly fishermen is to use a great variety of fly patterns and colors, but all in a similar size—usually around a size 10 to 14 hook because these are easy to see and to knot onto the leader. Most fly fishing experts agree that it's better to have fewer different patterns but in a greater variety of sizes. The average trout fisherman, for example, would be far better off with a fewer patterns but to have these in the size range from 8 to 18.

ATTACHING FLOSS

The quickest and surest way to attach floss, yarn, or similar fly body material is to fold the tag end of the stuff around the tying thread and make two or three tight winds of thread to hold the floss neatly and securely in place. No slipping, no pulling out when you start to wind, and the result is a smooth body on your fly.

MAKING DISPLAY PATTERNS BEHAVE

You have created the perfect fly for your display frame, but something doesn't seem right. The Spey hackle droops, the streamer wings sag, the tail just doesn't want to lay flat. The solution to these problems may be an application of non-lacquer, unscented hair spray. Spritz the fly with a small amount of the spray and hold the offending part in place for the few seconds it takes to dry. If the final result is not to your liking, steam out the hair spray and try again. You can try using a lacquer spray or fixative, but the results will be permanent.

CUTTING SHEET LATEX

To cut sheet latex into neat narrow strips, try this. Secure the sheet latex to a piece of cardboard using double-faced adhesive tape. Inexpensive tape that works well is used for laying carpets. After you make your cardboard-tape-latex sandwich, and using a metal straightedge, cut the latex into strips with a utility knife. This procedure can be adapted to other materials which requires cutting into narrow strips, but is too flexible or too bulky for the usual methods.

CUTTING LATEX

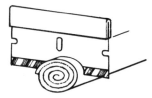

Cutting uniform strips of latex for nymphs can be difficult, as the material tends to bunch and "walk away" from the scissors. An easier method is to roll the latex sheet tightly and with a razor blade cut off slices in the widths that you require.

GOOD THEN, GOOD NOW

Over time, good ideas tend to resurface. Past issues of fishing magazines and old books contain many excellent fly-tying tips. Tyers who have been at it for some years should reread some of these resources. The chances are good that solutions to your fly-tying problems are already in print, and the search for them can become a thoroughly enjoyable hobby in itself.

DOUBLING HACKLE

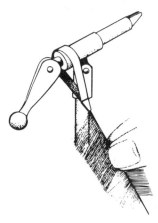

This tip is good for folding saddle hackle when tying Atlantic-salmon flies, but might be applied to other materials as well.

1. Trim a bare spot (1/4") near the tip of a hackle.

2. With open loop hackle pliers grab the hackle tip and slip the pliers over the handle of the vise.

3. Hold the hackle butt in your right hand, bright side forward, and dip your left index and thumb into a mixture of warm water and Ivory liquid soap.

4. With the left hand, fold the hackle fibers back. Start at the tip end and proceed toward the butt, wetting fingers as needed.

5. Tie in the hackle by the bare spot near the tip, with the tip tied under the hook and the folded fibers pointing up, and then wrap. Leave a blood feather at the base of the stem to help denote the back side of the saddle hackle.

LOOSE HAIR GRIP

If, when tying a batch of streamers, you occasionally let your mind wander and suddenly find a clump of bucktail clutched between thumb and forefinger about three steps before you need it, read on.

98

Placing the clump on the table usually results in bits and pieces of trimmings adhering to the hair—and what you laid down is not always what you pick up, for the strands of hair seem to have a will of their own.

Solve this problem by lining the inner jaws of a spring-loaded paper clamp with self-adhesive weather stripping. The sponge-like material has more than enough resiliency to envelop all of the hair and keep it firmly under control.

THUMBS DOWN

Thumb nails, that is. If putting streamer wings on so that they lie straight along the shank of the hook without cocking up or slipping off to one side is a problem, nick the stem of the feathers with your thumb nail right where the first turn of thread will lie, and then flatten the ends of the stem by drawing your thumbnail along their length. You'll find that the wings will sit on top of the shank just as straight as can be.

PINKING FEATHERS

If you tie a lot of nymphs, then you probably use a lot of pheasant "church window" feathers for their wing cases. Know how to trim these feathers to shape quickly and evenly? With pinking shears! Borrow these from a sewing basket, and you'll find it's not even necessary to fold the feather in half in order to cut the end to the "V" shape so many nymph patterns call for.

MAKING VARIEGATED CHENILLE

In tying the ubiquitous "Brindle Bug," the most-used steelhead fly for Klamath River summer steelhead, finding a source of variegated chenille may be difficult.

The Brindle Bug's standard tie is with a yellow-and-black variegated-chenille body; but, sometimes yellow and dark brown, tan and dark green, or green and black are more effective.

You can make your own by twisting together a strand of yellow chenille, and a strand of black. Lo-and-behold, they make instant variegated chenille, and stay together even when the twisting pressure is released.

Another bonus is the twisted chenille makes a much tighter full body. (Some commercial chenille is pretty skinny).

The inventory problem is solved. Simply carry the basic colors, and twist them together to make any combination desired.

The procedure is simple:

1. Place hook in vise, attach and wrap thread back to tail position above barb.

2. Place light and dark chenille parallel to each other, strip a 1/4" end of each strand down to core thread and bind to hook shank. Advance thread to forward end of desired body length.

3. Grasp both ends of chenille in hackle pliers and twist clockwise until "variegated" to suit.

4. Wind chenille forward in tight wraps for body length desired. Bind the ends with thread and clip away the excess chenille.

REALISTIC TRIPLE TAILS

With the current trend towards realism, more and more tyers are using peccary, moose mane, pheasant and other natural materials for tailing nymphs and dries. Synthetic fibers have also gained in popularity and are now offered in a wide variety of colors. Keeping these tails splayed and separated is one of the secrets of a good looking fly. Here's how:

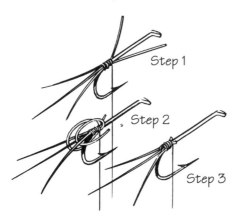

1. Tie in three tail fibers leaving the butts free. Clip the butt of the center fiber only, or disregard it.

2. Separate the fibers of the outer two tails and tuck the butts in as shown.

3. Snug up the outer two butts which will in turn separate and flare the fibers. Once you have achieved the flare you want, make a few wraps of thread over the butts to hold them in place.

If you are into realism, or just like the looks of a fly tied with three tails, give it a try.

MARABOU

When tying in marabou for tails or wings, wetting the clump of feathers makes it a lot easier to handle, and allows you to determine quite accurately the length, shape and density. A little extra quantity and length of marabou won't hurt. The material is soft enough to be torn off to the exact length and shape desired, using only your fingers, either at the bench or at streamside.

HANDLING TINY HACKLE

Use your hackle pliers when searching for a tiny (#20-#28) feather. The pliers are smaller than your fingertips so it's easier to latch onto just one feather. Then run your fingers down the selected feather to the base to remove it from the neck. Using hackle pliers also makes tying in this wee feather a good deal easier.

STEAM CLEANING

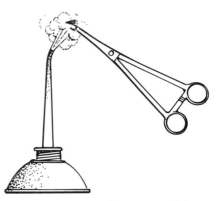

Have you ever tried to steam old, matted and dirty flies over a tea kettle? It works if the flies are only slightly matted, but the really messed up ones need more steam pressure than can be had from a kettle to return them to fishable condition. One solution is to use an oil can. Fill the can with water and bring to the boil on the stove. Use forceps to hold the fly in the steam or your pinkies will get pinker. For a portable model, use a small Sterno stove. Take care to keep the hole in the can clear and unplugged or you will be in for a real demonstration of the power of that steam!

DRYING WET FLIES

It is almost inevitable that at some time a box of flies will get a soaking.

A box of flies represents not only a lot of time, but also materials and hooks that will be ruined if not dried quickly. The problem is solved by placing a window screen over the opened boxes and turning a hair dryer on them. The screen prevents the flies from escaping their compartments and in next to no time the flies and boxes are completely dry, good as new and not rusted.

THE FOUNDATION WRAP

A hook shank wound with tying thread from eye to bend in snug, close wraps is the proper foundation for every good fly. There is no good reason to shirk this task when it can be done quickly and easily, here's how:

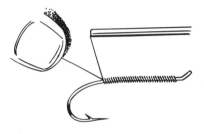

1. With hook in vise and bobbin in right hand the left hand pulls about three inches of thread from the bobbin and holds it snugly. The bobbin makes one turn over the hook shank and around toward the eye, then two snug turns over and around to the left, locking the thread.

2. At this point, instead of clipping off the tag end, hold it tight in a pinch between left thumb and forefinger, angling the tag above the hook shank and a little to the left at a high angle. Hold tight about an inch above the shank.

3. With bobbin tube held parallel to and about an inch above the hook shank, make widely spaced clockwise turns around the shank to the left. The thread from the bobbin should strike the angled tag end at the top of each turn, then slide down the angled tag to butt closely to the previous turn.

4. There is no need to carefully butt each turn or even to watch it closely. If both threads are held tightly the thread will lay on as closely as it does on its own spool.

5. When you reach the bend, let the bobbin hang. Pull up sharply on the tag end as you cut it off close at the point where it emerges from the wrap. The natural elasticity of the thread will bury the cut end under the last wrap.

6. Letting the bobbin hang, get out your magnifying glass and admire the best and quickest thread foundation you ever made.

RECYCLING MARABOU

Flies we tie and fish with most often, such as Alaskan and steelhead patterns and wooly buggers, require a lot of marabou in them. We have found that after tying in the uniform marabou plumes—as you would in a wooly bugger tail—there is still usable marabou left on most plumes. On these leftover pieces, stroke the loose marabou forward to an even point and pinch off the ends with your thumb and forefinger. This will result in a nice even taper in the plume that can be used again in wings and tails. Occasionally you may have to cut out the center stem if it is thick or inflexible.

TEACHING TIP

When teaching fly-tying classes bring some cord or twine or small ropes to teach the method of attaching thread to the hook, and also to teach the two-finger whip finish. Use the tying vise to simulate the hook and start the cord near the back to show how to tie the thread on the hook. Winding the cord up the vise demonstrate how to apply the whip finish with the larger cord. Using a cord with a color that contrasts with the vise color, and the larger cord, makes it easier to see than to use a fine black thread. Students should learn the whip finish at the first lesson and the cord will help accomplish that.

COLORED PEARLESCENT BODIES

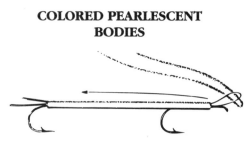

The use of Mylar braid in the construction of tandem streamers presents many problems. One concerns the use of pearlescent braid. To make different colored bodies for any fly using this material, colored yarn or tinsel must be pulled through the Mylar body after it has been threaded onto the hooks. To do this without difficulty, use a loop of 12 lb. coated, braided wire. It is stiff enough yet small enough in diameter to be threaded through the braided Mylar tube without fuss, and the yarn adds color under the fish scale flash of the Mylar.

TYING SLIPPERY MATERIALS

Streamer wings made of Flashabou, or other similar slippery materials, tend to pull out from the head after repeated attacks from fish. A simple solution is to double the strands of Flashabou over themselves during tying.

For a wing of six strands, for example, cut three strands of material, twice the length required. Tie these in at their center and, once secured in place, the forward ends can be folded back and tied down. The Flashabou, now trapped by the tying thread, will not pull out.

NEATNESS COUNTS

Having difficulty with tying a neat tapered tinsel tip on your flies? Especially 5the ones calling for oval tinsel? After tying in the tinsel, untwist your tying thread until it lays flat on the hook. For a righthanded tyer, this means twisting the bobbin in a counterclockwise direction. Lay your turns of the tying thread on the hook so that each one touches the previous one until there is just room for one turn of tinsel on the bare hook. Rewind the tying thread two or three turns back toward the eye of the hook, taking care to unwind the thread so that it lays very flat on the hook shank. Carefully wind the tinsel, (remember, first turn should be on the bare shank), and you'll find that by having flattened your tying thread, the second turn of tinsel will lay neatly on the thread, with no unsightly step-up or gap. The drawing shows the difference between normally twisted, and untwisted tying thread. And, of course, use extra fine oval or #16/18 flat mylar tinsel for all tips. The fine oval or #14 flat is simply too wide for a really tidy tip.

TO AVOID GIARDIA (BEAVER FEVER)

Don't put your thumb in your mouth to moisten your fingers for dubbing—you don't know what that rabbit slept with last.

A small bowl with a few pieces of sponge cut to fit and moistened with water makes a more sanitary method for wetting your fingers when dubbing.

STOPPING SLIPPAGE

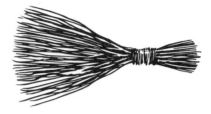

How to keep a floss or wool body or tag from slipping down over the tip? Here's how. Tie your floss or wool on top of the hook, leaving an inch or two hanging at the rear of the hook. Wind the tag or body as usual, and tie off this working end at the bottom of the hook. Then take the piece of material now hanging at the top rear, make certain that it is not twisted, lay it over the top of the wound floss or wool, using a bit of tension to make it lie neatly on top of the hook, and tie it down with a couple of turns of thread. Voilà, the tag is going to stay where you tied it with no untidy slippage down over the tinsel, and the result is a neat and more durable fly.

LIGHTWEIGHT DRY FLIES
To minimize the addition of weight and bulk, especially on your dry flies, remember to never take two turns of thread when one turn will do the job. Also, don't add a turn to do the job which the previous turn should have been made to do.

TAG ENDS
Leave a tag end of the thread when tying divided wing dries. Start by putting on the wings and use the tag end to separate and divide the wings to have more control then when using the bobbin for dividing the wings. If you forget, you can tie in a dubbing loop and butt the thread for a tag end, then divide and bind in the end with the bobbin.

Also use the tag end for rein-forcing herl bodies by counter winding the herl with the tag end, then binding down with the bobbin.

TAILING MATERIAL

On flies tied with tail fibers such as moose, or elk mane, cut a large bunch of hair, remove the fluff from the base with a dubbing needle, place the hair into a stacker and even the ends, remove the stacked hair and bind the bundle with tying thread. When you need a tail, separate a few of the hairs for the job and snip them off, no need to stack the hair for every fly. A large bundle will get you through a couple of dozen flies.

RIBBING BODIES

When adding a body ribbing such as tinsel, wire, stripped quill, or thread, it is a good idea to wrap it in a direction opposite to the winds of the body material. If the body was wound on clockwise, wrap the ribbing in a counterclockwise direction. This prevents the ribbing from sinking into the joints of the body, and can add a degree of protection against the fly body becoming frayed by sharp teeth.

SEPARATING GOOSE-BIOT TAILS

Goose biots are often used to simulate the tails of stone fly nymphs. They are flexible yet sturdy, and they can be dyed to match the color of most naturals. Most of the time, goose-biots curve naturally. Therefore, tyers can separate the goose-biot tail by tying a biot on each side of the shank at the bend so that the biot's natural bend is away from the shank.

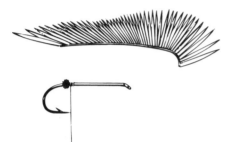

Tip #1. Tie in the chenille and make one wrap or tie in a little "ball" of dubbing fur at the bend of the hook.

Sometimes goose-biots are almost straight and the biots won't curve naturally away from the shank like we want them to. When this happens, don't tie the biots in at the bend of the hook. Tie in the chenille and make one wrap, or, if the body is dubbed fur, form a little "ball" of material right at the bend of the hook. Then tie in a biot on each side of the shank. The single wind of chenille of the ball or dubbing will force the biots to separate.

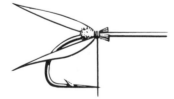

Tip #2. Tie in the goose biots starting with the biot on the far side of the shank. The protrusion caused by the

single wrap of chenille or the little "ball" of dubbing fur will separate the goose-biots and make them curve away from the hook. It's also easier to tie them both the same length.

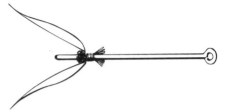

By the way, separation is never a problem when biots are used at the eye-end of the hook because the eye works like the wrap of chenille or ball of dubbing to separate the goose-biot "antennae".

TANDEM FLIES

To make an improved link connecting the hooks for tandem flies, take a piece of braided lead core line and remove the lead, replacing it with monofilament line of the same diameter. Here is a good combination to use:

Lead Core: 27 lb. test
Color: Red or orange
Mono: 15 lb. Maxima
Rear hook: Partridge Double
    Wilson size 14
Front hook: Mustad 38941 Size 6
Thread: Uni-Thread 6/0 red

This linkage works perfectly. It provides good flexibility and strength without slippage. The rear hook will stay balanced with the front one without kinking. All kinds of linkages have been tried: flat and round mono, stainless steel wire, seven stranded wire, nylon coated wire, double mono looped, lead core line, etc. and none of those matched the lead core and mono combination.

You can match the color of the thread wraps with the color of the lead core line, as most lead core lines are marked with different colors like green, blue, olive, red, orange, yellow, brown, white etc.

No need to use big thread or cement to bond the combination since the 6/0 Uni-Thread will get deep between the woven core line. Simply go back and forth once with your working thread, whip finish and apply lacquer.

The double hook will break before the linkage slips or breaks.

For best balance of the fly in the water, it's best to use a smaller hook at the rear and a larger one up front.

HACKLE SLIDING

Does your hackle slide off the back of your woolly worm? Try this tip.

Tie in the tail fibers, chenille and hackle (in that order). When you begin to wrap chenille up hook shank, first wrap one full turn of chenille behind the hackle. This will secure the hackle and prevent its sliding down around the bend of the hook. It also helps protect the hackle from being cut by the sharp teeth of a fish.

TOUGHEN FILOPLUMES

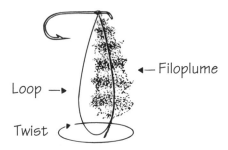

Filoplumes (aftershaft feathers) are very fragile. This is how to toughen them for fly tying.

1. Place a filoplume in an unwaxed dubbing loop and twist it.

2. Snap the thread with your finger as you twist. This will prevent the fibers from being wound down.

3. As you wind the filoplume on the fly, stroke the fibers back.

SIMPLER THREAD CUTS

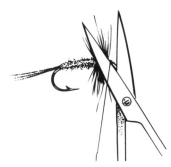

Some tyers slice their thread rather than cutting it with scissors. While holding the scissor blades very slightly open with one hand and pulling the thread taut with the other, push the scissor blades through the thread as close to the hook as possible. The thread is cut off under tension so that no objectionable short strand is left behind to show. This process is probably most valuable in finishing off the head of a dry fly. The thread under tension will be cut, but any stray hackle barbs will simply slip through the blades. But is is also useful in other steps where thread, floss, peacock, herl or various other materials need to be removed and where cutting might also take part or all of something you didn't want to remove.

PREVENT UNRAVELLING

In recent years flies with braided Mylar bodies have become very popular. Often, when threading the braid over the hook, the braid will unravel making a neat body almost impossible. Some braids are worse than others, even from the same supplier.

One solution is simple. Paint (don't dip) the end of the braid with thinned fingernail polish and let dry.

TRIMMED HACKLES

Unless you are tying flies to sell, or for their appearance, don't worry too much if you don't have hackle small enough for the dry fly you wish to construct.

Simply select a somewhat larger hackle with all the same properties of color and stiffness, wind it on, and trim it to the desired length with your scissors. Admittedly, the result won't win any contests or friends among the purists— but do you think the fish will notice? There have even been experts who argue that clipped hackle is superior.

SLIPPERY HAIR?

Wax →

Have you ever been frustrated by the slipperiness of calf hair?

Before snipping the calf hair from the hide, apply a dose of dubbing wax to the area of hair where it will be tied in—about a third of the distance from the hair root to the tip. Then cut a thin layer of hair.

The tips of the hair will stay fairly even, and with the wax the hair will stay together when tied and will not slip around the shaft of the hook.

STEAM INTO SHAPE

Feathers, and some furs, that have become curled, mashed, bent, or otherwise damaged can often be restored to good condition by holding them over live steam. An ordinary teapot will provide the steam, but take care not to scald your fingers. A pair of tongs will help avoid this problem.

DOUBLING MALLARD

Some salmon and steelhead fly patterns, called wet spiders, require a

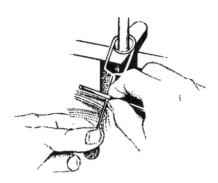

"doubled" hackle, often of mallard flank. Use an old pair of scissors to break down the left side (for right handed tyers) of a mallard hackle before doubling and tying in.

TRADE WITH HUNTERS

If you don't hunt, be sure to cultivate a barter arrangement with one of your hunting friends or acquaintances.

Offer to tie some flies, or perhaps repair an old rod, in exchange for some of those useful feathers which are not available for sale through commercial sources. Of greatest interest would be feathers from woodcock, grouse or crows. Many of the waterfowl feathers, like pintail, woodduck, and mallard are, of course, useful as well. Big game hunters, particularly deer and elk hunters, can provide you with an enormous quantity and variety of hair.

TIDY TINSEL TIE-INS

Large diameter oval tinsels are called for in many large salmon patterns. In order to cut down bulk at the tie-in point, strip off the tinsel for about 1/4 inch, exposing the silk core and tie that in, making certain that none of the core shows at the first wrap of the tag or rib.

HOLD THAT WIRE!

The fine wire used for tags or ribbing on small flies is very slippery and has a tendency to pull out. To prevent this from happening, tie it in with three or four wraps of thread and then fold the tag end back on itself and wrap it again. Finish the rib or tag the same way. It is now impossible for the wire to pull out, and the result is a much more durable fly. The wire is so fine, that almost no bulk is added by using this method.

FANNING SQUIRREL HAIR

When tying Trude-style flies, or any dry-fly pattern that calls for a squirrel hair wing, after tying in the wing, and before the cement used under the windings has set, pinch with tweezers or small pliers just behind the tie-in area to fan out the squirrel hair. This aids flotation and enhances the fish-taking ability of the fly.

WEED GUARDS
To keep your fly from getting hung up in snags, try any of these weed guards:

1. Single wire weed guard

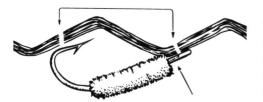

2. Synthetic rope weed guard

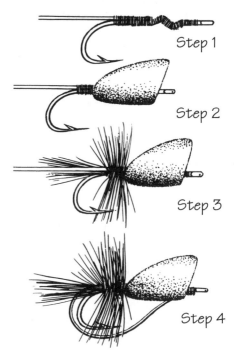

Step 1

Step 2

Step 3

Step 4

3. Nylon monofilament weed guard

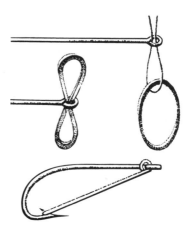

4. Emergency weed guard

MARRYING WITHOUT TEARS
When cutting slips for married wings on salmon flies, it is a big help to put the slips for each wing into small boxes marked "Left" and "Right". That way, there is far less opportunity for mixing them up, especially if you are interrupted while tying.

PULL-PROOF HACKLE

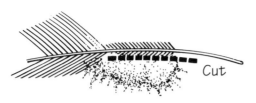

When preparing a hackle to be tied in, do not tear off the soft fluff at the base of the feather. Instead, cut the unwanted barbules, leaving just a bit of "fringe." Then, when the feather is tied in, the thread will bite between the barbule stubs and make it all but impossible to pull out the hackle. This technique is especially useful when tying in body veilings on certain full-dress salmon flies as it will help keep the veilings from twisting around instead of lying straight along the hook shank.

STRAIGHTEN UP AND SWIM RIGHT

When setting feather wings, it's a help to place them against the hook shank at about 11 o'clock so that the first turns of thread will bring them up on top of the hook where they belong, and not cocked off-center towards the far side of the hook shank.

SMOOOTH TINSEL

When tying salmon or streamer flies that have flat tinsel bodies, try winding an underbody, consisting of a layer or two of floss, on the hook shank before you wind the tinsel. The floss will even out any irregularities caused by previously tied-in materials, and make a fine smooth base for the tinsel.

BEFORE THE FLY IS FINISHED AND PUT ASIDE . . .

Make certain that the hook point is very sharp, using a small sharpening stone if necessary, and that the eye of the hook is free of varnish, hackle barbs, and anything else that might impede the easy passage of the leader. These are two of the signs of a well-tied fly.

TAMING TOPPINGS

One of the more recalcitrant materials that salmon-fly tyers use is the crest feather from the golden pheasant. When worn by the living bird, the crests are probably fairly straight and twist-free, but by the time it is purchased by the tyer the crest usually is not in such pristine condition. In order to use the long individual feathers for toppings, they must first be straightened so that they will lie neatly atop the wing, and even the shorter ones used for tails usually need a bit of straightening. There are several ways to accomplish this:

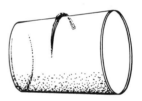

1. They can be wet and placed on the outside of a tumbler the diameter of which approximates the shape of the wing and let dry undisturbed.

2. The topping may be held in a pair of tweezers in the column of steam from a

tea kettle until the individual fibers and stem relax and assume a true curve.

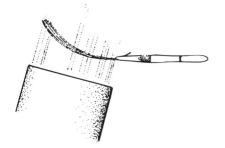

3. Again, using tweezers, the topping may be held in the path of a stream of hot air from a hair drier. The air should be directed down the topping, from the stem to the tip. This last method works well when the topping is not terribly out of shape. In the case of really badly twisted feathers, hot steam seems to work best.

STRAIGHT-UP STREAMER WINGS

In spite of using a "soft loop" when attaching streamer wings, some fly tyers find that saddle hackles, especially when using four or more feathers, tend to spin off-center towards the far side of the hook. To avoid this, half-hitch the tying thread and reverse wind it a couple of times. With the wings divided into near and far sides, take the far side saddles and attach them with reverse winds. Make another half-hitch and resume your normal winding direction to attach the near-side wings. This method insures that both wings have thread tension that tends to center them and keep them on top of the hook where they belong. Use fine thread to avoid bulk—the super-strength 8/0 thread is great.

GRASSHOPPERS GROW

Grasshoppers start out in life pretty small—somewhere about a size 20 as a guess—but as the season wears on they grow. A full-grown healthy hopper is imitated on about a size 4 or 6 hook. If you fish these very productive patterns, why not imitate life, and tie them in a number of sizes, using the smaller ones early in the season, and gradually increase the size you use as the summer wears on.

STREAMLINED WEED GUARD

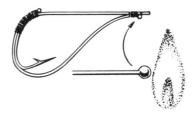

Attach the monofilament weed guard at the bend of the hook in the conventional manner, then tie and trim the bug. When you are finished trimming, bring the mono weed guard to the hook eye as usual and cut off, leaving 1/16" of mono past the eye. Hold the end of the mono away from the bug and with a cigarette lighter melt the end to form a small bead. Insert the bead into the eye of the hook and make two or three snug wraps with 6/0 thread behind the eye. Pull the bead back until it stops against the thread wraps and whip finish.

This method gives you an unobstructed eye and a much neater head than other methods.

FOR SMOOTH FINGERS

One item that should be on your fly tying desk is a strip of fine emery cloth. Sold in 9" X 11" sheets, rip it lengthwise into 2" strips. Then, clasping between thumb and forefinger, smooth your fingertips by pulling gently downward against the cloth with the opposite hand. Now, threads and flosses no longer fray against rough skin, and the emery cloth lasts a long time.

FLATTENED CHENILLE

When tying flies that require chenille, the chenille is often matted and smashed making it difficult to tie a neat looking fly. This is especially true if the chenille has been wound on cards.

Unwind the chenille from the card and hold it for a few seconds over a steaming tea kettle. The steam will fluff up the chenille like new.

COVERED HOOK POINTS

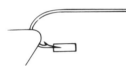

Often, beginning tyers (and not a few pros) break their tying thread when it brushes against a sharp hook point. The best way to avoid that problem is learning to miss the point through experience. As an extra measure of security place a small piece of Larva Lace on the hook point. The soft plastic material is hollow and easily fits over the sharpened point. If the tying thread hits the covered area no damage is done. Just remember to remove the plastic before using the pattern on fish!

WET FLOSS FRAYS LESS

Do you find that tying with floss reveals each and every rough spot on your hands by becoming increasingly frayed with each turn around the hook shank? Try this. Simply wet the floss before wrapping it. That's all it takes to reduce or eliminate fraying, and your fly will dry in no time.

SHOOT THAT FLY!

Most tyers are constantly striving to improve their tying techniques, the proportions of their flies, the overall professional "look" of their work. A magnifying glass is something of a help to this end, but far better is the use of a "macro" lens on a camera. Take pictures of both sides of your best fly, focusing so that the fly just about fills the camera's viewfinder. Have the resulting shot blown up to at least 8" x 10" and you will be astounded (and shocked) at the imperfections in your perfect fly—hackle barbs astray, the wing just a smidge long, a tiny stub of tying thread left at the head, thread windings showing through the varnish. This is a very good (but humbling) method of measuring your tying progress.

WASTE NOT, WANT NOT

Are you planning to tie more than one fly using the same color of wool, chenille or similar material? Most tyers cut a 4" piece, but use only 2" in the fly, throw away the remainder, and then cut another 4" piece to repeat the process. You can save a lot of material by starting with a longer piece of material and using it repeatedly. Instead of six 4" pieces (24" total) for a half-dozen flies, all that's needed is one 14" piece.

PRO TYERS MUST PAY

Just a reminder to keep everyone out of trouble with Uncle Sam. Tax law requires that anyone who derives income from the manufacture of fishing tackle, including flies, must pay a federal excise tax—this includes hand tied flies. For complete information contact the Internal Revenue Service.

PROTECT YOUR TAIL

When tying leeches, Woolly Buggers, rabbit-strip patterns or marabou flies, if, after you tie the tail on the fly, you wrap a piece of tin foil over it, tying the rest of the fly is a lot easier.

MARVELOUS MARABOU

What a wonderful streamer wing marabou makes! It breathes and pulsates in the water, and few fish can resist it. Its one drawback is its propensity for wrapping itself around the body of the fly. To avoid this tie in a hackle feather of approximately the same color as the marabou you plan to use, at the rear of the hook. Bring your tying thread forward to the head of the fly. Palmer the hackle along the hook shank and tie off at the head. Clip the hackle fibers from the bottom and sides of the hook and clip a V in the hackle along the top of the hook, forming a sort of trough into which the marabou wing will nestle when you tie it in. This method seems to keep the marabou parallel to the hook shank when casting, except in terribly windy conditions.

AW SHUCKS - IT'S PLASTIC

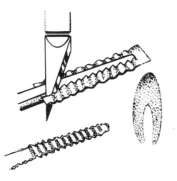

Clamp a rectangle of fairly heavy plastic in the jaws of a hemostat and trim around the jaws, leaving a small margin of plastic showing. Run a flame around the jaws which will melt back the plastic. When you remove it from the hemostat, you'll see that a bead has been formed around the edge, and that the impression of the jaws is molded into the plastic's surface.

Remove the tip end of the plastic and cut inside each bead for a short distance, then cut out the center strip, but don't discard it. The two-tailed piece that you've made makes a super stonefly or other two-tailed nymph. The center scrap that you saved can be used for a nymphal shuck. And by melting two pieces of plastic together, a segmented tube will be formed—a shuck with thickness as well as length and width. Because it's hollow it can be filled with any number of materials.

TAMING FEATHERWINGS

When tying feather winged streamers, the feathers often can be persuaded to match, even if they're all "rights" or "lefts." Take a hackle, place the quill across your thumbnail and gently pull the feather across your nail. The more pressure applied, the greater the arc obtained. Do the same thing with the feather for the other side. If you've used equal pressure, the feathers should cup together nicely

BUG LEGS

The conventional method of attaching rubber legs to bass bugs—tying each one around the hook shank as you build the deer hair body—has many drawbacks, not least of which is the number of times a leg is accidentally cut off while you're trimming the hair. Here's a method that's worked well for me. Spin on the deer hair and trim to shape. Tie two overhand knots 1/8" apart in the center of the rubber strips. Using a needle threader, thread end of rubber through a stout sewing needle and push the needle into the bug. Apply a bit of Pliobond between the knots and pull through the bass bug until the two knots straddle the hook shank. This method puts the legs just where you want them, and has the added advantage of being replaceable, should a vicious bass sever some of them!

TOUGH TENT-WINGS

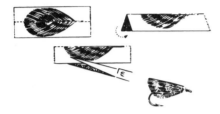

Tent-wing patterns are among the most successful for trout, their only drawback being the fragility of the wing. However, if you first stick the bottom side of the feather onto a piece of transparent mending tape (the kind that looks kind of whitish and can be written on), then fold the tape/feather assembly on the feather's center line and trim to the shape you want, you'll have a really durable wing that may outlast the rest of the fly. I make up a number of these wings at a sitting using different sizes, different feathers. They work very well indeed.

PERFECT WINGS
Here's a technique for evenly dividing hair or feather fiber dry fly wings and making the figure 8 wrap easier and more precise. With the wing material tied in, divide the fibers into two equal clumps with the point of the bodkin held parallel to the hook shank, and hold the bodkin in place. Now wind the thread figure 8 style once over the bodkin shank and the wing clump. Slowly withdraw the bodkin, maintaining thread tension, and finish the figure 8 wraps. The result is evenly divided wings, both in the amount of material in each, and the spread between them.

SKINNY TINSEL
I use pearl tinsel in the large size for wing cases on Flashback nymphs. Recently I've discovered how to decrease the width of this material so it can also be used for ribbing on some patterns. Simply grasp each end of a strand of tinsel and gently stretch it. The width will reduce from 3/32" to about 1/32".

POPPING CLEAN POPPERS
The best way to paint cork and balsa wood poppers is to dip them. However, the hook eye usually gets clogged with paint and in its removal the eye ends up looking less than neat. To solve this problem, prepare the hooks by dipping the eye into the hot wax surrounding the wick of a lit candle before you dip the popper into the paint. You'll find that the paint doesn't stick to the wax very well, and when dry, it can easily be scraped off with a toothpick. This simple trick results in a beautiful paint job and a professional looking paint-free eye.

TAMING MARABOU
There are a number of problems in handling dry marabou: everything from rough hands to static electricity. Dampening the marabou makes handling it a whole lot easier. I keep a small pump spray bottle on my tying table which once held lens cleaner and is now filled with water. Its fine mist controls the marabou very well. Works lots easier than dipping your hand in a bowl of water, and certainly light years better than running the marabou between your lips to moisten it.

LILY GILDING
To dress up your bass poppers start by heating a dubbing needle and burning

or melting holes in the hard plastic bodies. Once the holes are made, such goodies as rubber legs and mono loop weed guards can be inserted and then held firmly in place by the judicious use of Superglue. Both the hole burning and the gluing should be done in a well-ventilated area to avoid inhaling the fumes, and take care not to burn your fingers.

PLASTIC TUBING FOR THUNDER CREEKS

Clear plastic tubing is available at most hardware stores for pennies per foot. Cut off about a 2" section and use as a bullet head tool for tying Thunder Creek series streamers. The stuff is clear so that very accurate placement of the tie-down point is possible.

EASY HUMPIES

Humpies, or Goofus Bugs, are not the easiest of flies to construct but here's a tip that may help. After tying in the tail fibers, Scotch tape them to the vise. Then, when collecting the deer hair to form the "hump," there's no need to separate the tail hair from the body hair. When the fly is finished, carefully remove the tape. This procedure has saved endless aggravation.

TEARLESS MATUKAS

If you alway have problems tying Matuka streamers and spent a lot of time with a dubbing needle trying to make the feather on top look right, start using a sewing needle. Run the braid or thread through the eye of the needle and then sew through the feather as close as possible to the stem. This method saves a lot of fiddling and the feather looks better, too.

SEPARATING COLORS ON BUCKTAILS

To avoid mixing the colors of two or three color bucktail or calf hair wings, or having the hair creep around the hook shank instead of staying on top like it's supposed to, try making a complete turn of tying thread around each color before you tie it onto the shank. This trick works not only for this application, but also for tying upright hair wings on dry flies such as Wulffs.

BACKWINDING

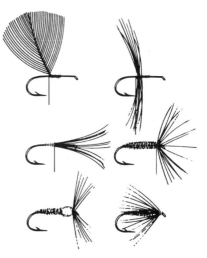

Ever wish you had an endless supply of partridge feathers in size 14 and 16? Perhaps you already do. By using a hackle winding technique that I call back winding, feathers that appear to be 8s and 10s effectively become 14s and smaller. To tie a typical soft hackle wet fly in size 14, first secure a feather to the hook about halfway back towards the bend. Next, wind it 1 1/2 or two times around the shank, tie it off and bring the thread forward to the eye. Next, carefully fold the barbules forward to the hook eye, tie off, and move thread back to the bend. Attach floss or other body material, then move thread forward again to the thorax area. Wind the floss to form the body and dub a fur thorax. Then, using a half hitch tool, push the barbules back over the body, form a neat thread head, and tie off. And there you have a well-proportioned soft hackle, using feathers once discarded!

THE COMPUTER COMES TO THE TYING TABLE

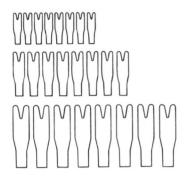

Many patterns, such as shrimp, crayfish and stonefly nymphs, call for cutting some form of sheet material into exact shapes. The desktop home computer can be a great help in preparing the materials. Using a painting or drawing program you can design on screen the shape you desire. This shape can then be scaled, either on screen or while printing, to provide you with the various sizes needed. Next, print the patterns on adhesive backed paper, such as large mailing labels. The patterns are then stuck onto the flat sheet fly-tying material you wish to use, and the shape is easily cut out with scissors. Using this system you can readily provide yourself with a large supply of consistent shapes.

PROBLEM-FREE ZONKERS

When tying Zonkers, one encounters three problems: first, making the lead wire used for weight slip-free; second, shaping the body; and third, durability. All three problems are solved by covering the lead with yarn prior to putting on the Mylar tubing. After wrapping the lead onto the shank of the hook, attach the yarn at the eye, wrap to the bend of the hook, follow the yarn with the tying thread, and then wrap back up to the eye with the yarn and then the thread. The thread adds amazing durability. Shaping can be accomplished by twisting and untwisting the yarn. This method works well for shaping the thorax on large nymphs and stoneflies, too. For Zonkers use emerald green yarn under translucent pearl Mylar tubing for a realistic minnow body.

NEAT PAIRS

When tying feather-tailed flies such as Lefty's Deceiver, first match several pairs of feathers. An easy way to keep them paired is to catch the base of each set of feathers between a sheet of "Post-It" notes, available in any stationery store. Fold the sheet sticky side in and the paired feathers will be securely held until needed.

MATCHED WINGS

When tying muddlers or other flies with quill wings, clamp a hook of the size you're tying into a forceps. Then use the gape of this hook to measure, then separate, the quill section for the wing before clipping it. The result is evenly paired wings of the correct height.

TIP FOR TYING TEACHERS

A common problem for fly tying students is the difficulty of seeing what the instructor is doing while nine or ten of them jockey for position looking over his shoulders. Using a video camcorder hooked to a portable TV to enlarge the fly, students can easily view all the steps. The camcorder is set on a small box on the tying table and the vise is then adjusted for height. Set the camcorder on MACRO and focus it. Hook the camcorder to the TV input with the same cord you use for direct viewing. This will enlarge the fly to about 12 inches on a 19 inch screen. If you have a color TV, so much the better, but a black and white will serve as well.

An added feature is that as you are able to control the TV volume, you don't have to raise your voice to explain things or answer questions. Your students are able to hear you as well as see what you are doing.

BIOT BEHAVIOR

When tying a goose biot in by the tip for a fly body, keeping the notch at the base to the left will produce a smooth body, whereas the notch facing to the right will produce a fuzzier, segmented body. Soaking the biot in water to which a drop of hair conditioner has been added will make it easier to wind.

MYLAR PIPING
THAT BEHAVES

The cure for unbraiding ends of Mylar piping is to brush a light coat of Dave's Flexament along one edge. First remove the core, then cement and let dry, being careful that the Mylar braid doesn't collapse. Do about a foot at a time.

EASY GLUING OF BASS BUGS

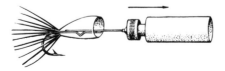

If you have trouble with the glue squirting out of the back of the slide-on foam heads for bass bugs, try using one of the plastic applicator bottles that has a long tube on the front end. Slide the tube into the foam head from the front end back to the tail of the bug. Start to pull the tube forward slowly as you squeeze out the glue. The glue will neatly fill in any gaps that may have occurred when you slid the head on over the materials.

ON THE WATER

"Trout are the ultimate judges and they can at times be stern taskmasters."

Chauncy Lively
Chauncy Lively's Flybox, 1980

SWIZZLE-STICK NAIL KNOTTER

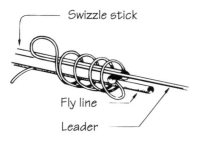

The double-tubed swizzle stick/coffee stirrer makes a perfect tool for nail knots. The double tubes have an indented connection, making it simple to wrap the leader butt end over fly line tip and tubes the number of turns desired. Then pass the leader end through the indented section connecting the tubes for a neat and well-proportioned nail knot.

ONE MORE ITEM FOR YOUR VEST

Even though you are already carrying enough fly boxes, leader spools, scales, bug dope, flotant etc., in your vest, make room for one of the small nets that home aquarium keepers use. They cost about a dollar and are small enough and light enough not to take up much room or add much weight to your already overloaded vest. If you fish water where the trout are extra-selective, the net will pay for itself many times over. By seining some of the nymphs and emergers you'll be able to match the current food of choice and will increase your catch significantly. And if you have room in your vest for a couple of screw-top vials, you can save the insects and tie pretty darned good imitations with which to fool the trout. If you keep records of which insects were taken when, you can create an entire hatching schedule for your river which will serve for many years to come.

THREADING MIDGE HOOKS

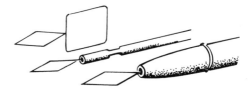

Ball-point pens may run out of ink but not out of usefulness. Try gluing a needle threader (the kind you find in sewing kits) onto the end of an empty ball point ink cartridge. Miracle glue works well. Replace the cartridge into the pen which should have a spring retractor. You now have a tool to insert tippets through midge hook eyes. Helpful for those of us who no longer enjoy 20/20 vision. Looks like a pen in your vest pocket.

SAMPLES JAR

If you keep in your fishing vest a small rugged bottle, jar, or better yet, a 35mm film canister, then you will have the ability to capture insect samples while fishing. You can then bring home these samples where they can be identified so you're able to tie the appropriate imitations. They can also serve as models for your flies.

SAFETY-PIN GUIDE

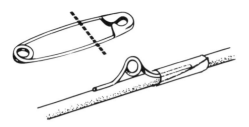

In an emergency a common safety pin can be pressed into service as a fly rod guide. Simply cut off the clasp head and the point, and bend the two ends outwards. They can be wound on with thread or in a pinch, taped in place. The loop of the safety pin is very smooth so the fly line's finish won't be harmed, and its diameter is large enough for the heaviest line.

END DISPENSER HASSLE

Loading some of the leader dispensers that have the small spools can be a real hassle, but here is a very neat solution. Use a rechargeable screwdriver! Just slip the dispenser spool over the bit, and wind away. If you hold the factory spool in your other hand, you can control the tension very easily. Works like a charm!

A WISE PRECAUTION

Nylon leader material, especially in very fine sizes, should be carefully examined, and tested by pulling it in proportion to the weight expected to be held by it. This precaution will frequently prevent the loss of a fish by discovering a weak spot in the material before, rather than after, the fact.

SIZE - SHAPE - COLOR

Many of your top anglers would agree that when it comes to selecting a fly the most important considerations are size, shape and color—in that order. By shape we mean the fly form such as slim or stout, upright wing or down wing, and so forth. A sure sign of a beginning fly fisherman is a box of flies in a rainbow of colors—but all tied on size 12 hooks. You are far better off with fewer colors, possibly just light, medium and dark, but in a wide range of sizes, and with some variety in silhouette (shape) as well.

TIPPET DISPENSER

Make your own tippet dispenser out of an empty dental-floss dispenser.

It can be very frustrating trying to find the end of your tippet spool. This new dispenser eliminates that problem. Pry open the floss container, tape one end of your tippet material to the wheel and wind it on clockwise. Then thread the tippet through the guide hole and across to the cutter.

Be sure to label your tippet data on the plain side of the dispenser with a permanent marker.

GOOD FISHERMEN
ARE GOOD OBSERVERS

Become an observer of your flies. Don't be satisfied with how they appear at your tying bench. Take them to the stream. Before casting to a fish lay the flies in the water beside you. Observe how they float or sink, how they move, how the tippet affects them, and how they appear. By doing this you'll often find yourself back at the tying bench seeking improvement and in the long run catching more fish.

COLD-HAND KNOTS

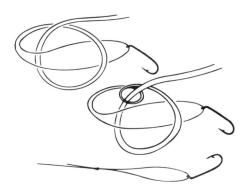

We've all experienced the frustration of trying to tie a fly onto fine tippet with cold and clumsy fingers. The solution is to use a Surgeon's end loop knot. The drawings speak louder than words. Suffice it to say that I have had no pullouts or other types of knot failures using this method and the fly swinging loose and moving in the current (a la the Duncan Loop knot) makes for a very natural presentation.

TYING ONE ON

If you are having trouble tying a midge or other small fly onto your leader when the light starts to go, a good trick is to take a half dozen or so of these tiny flies and pre-tie them to lengths of tippet. It's a lot easier to tie a barrel or double surgeon's knot at dusk than it is to try and thread fine tippet through the eye of a size 18 hook.

CLEAR LABELS

The clear, self-stick address labels that are available at most stationers are great for putting your name and address on your fly boxes. If by some misfortune a box falls out of your vest streamside, most fishermen are honest folks and will return it, if only they know to whom it belongs.

DRYING WET FLIES

It is almost inevitable that at some time a box of flies will get a soaking. A box of flies represents not only a lot of time, but also materials and hooks that will be ruined if not dried quickly.

The problem is solved by placing a window screen over the opened boxes and turning a hair dryer on them. The screen prevents the flies from escaping their compartments and in next to no time the flies and boxes will be completely dry and as good as new, with no rust on the hooks.

ANOTHER IMPROVEMENT

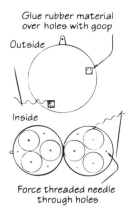

Glue rubber material over holes with goop

Outside

Inside

Force threaded needle through holes

The Dennison Leader Dispenser is a compact, durable and inexpensive item for carrying tippet material astream. Its drawbacks are its inability to keep the working ends of tippet secure, and difficulty in identifying the various tippet sizes. Both these problems can be remedied. From rubber gasket material about 1/16" thick, cut six 1/4" squares. Glue these over the holes in the dispenser with Sportsman's Goop and let dry. Thread the end of the leader material through a sewing needle and from the inside of the dispenser, force the needle through the gasket. Not only will this securely hold the ends of the tippets, but the leader is straightened as you draw it through the rubber. Mark the tippet sizes on small pieces of masking tape and stick each one next to the corresponding size of tippet.

BELLY-BOAT FLY STORAGE

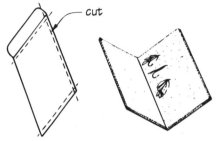

When fishing from a float tube some anglers prefer the added safety of wearing a life jacket, so a vest is not practical. Thus one becomes dependent on the storage pockets built into the tube to stow his tackle.

By cutting a 6" x 8" foam-lined mailing envelope as shown, a good inexpensive container for storing flies results. Three edges of the envelope are trimmed away and then it is cut in half. The resulting fly folders can be marked with their contents and flies are hooked into the foam of the folders. Several of these neat folders can be placed in a Zip-Loc bag and several bags can be stowed in the side pockets of the tube cover.

The envelopes cost about 30 cents each, making the cost per folder a dirt-cheap 15 cents. Another plus is that they float!

TIGHT TIPPET SPOOLS

The nuisance of trying to keep the loose ends of tippet material from unwinding in your fishing-vest pocket is a first-class nuisance. The rubber bands or plastic clips that are supplied with each spool are a long way from satisfactory and the fancy multi-weight tippet holders are expensive and time consuming to load. Try using "pony-

tail" elastics found in drug or notions stores. These elastic-and-fabric hair-control items are very inexpensive and come in a variety of colors, which is helpful for determining the line strength in low light. Best of all, no more trailing ends of tippet from your vest!

ON-THE-WATER FLY FIX

After you tie your masterpiece and get a chance to fish it, you may find that it doesn't swim exactly as you hoped— it's upside down, it spins, it rides on its side, or it has any other number of problems. For future flies adjustments need to be considered, such as size and weight of hook, choice and amount of materials, etc. But if you want to fish your fly now, here's a quick fix. A small amount of very fine solder wrapped on the bend of the hook and held in place with a drop of super glue might be all that's needed to make your fly track properly.

Another fix, though one that runs the risk of breaking the hook, is to bend the eye up at approximately 45 degrees. This may correct the problem.

TABBING AN ELASTIC BAND

Trying to grasp the elastic band that most of us use to keep a spool of tippet material from unwinding is a real pain unless the band has a tab or "ear" on it. However, if you tie a granny knot in a rubber band, voila - an easy to grasp tag.

SLICK SPLICES

An excellent method of joining fly line to leader butt is to glue them together. Here's how.

Cut the fly line cleanly behind the old nail knot, and with a sewing needle having approximately the diameter of the leader butt work the sharp end of the needle into the center or core of the fly line as far as it will go, usually 3/16 to 1/4 inch. Repeat this procedure four or five times to ensure that the end of the fly line is really stretched out. Heating the needle before inserting it into the fly line also helps stretch the center of the line. Then prepare the leader by cutting the butt end at about a 45 ° angle and roughen up the surface of the last 1/4 inch or so of the nylon, using a hook hone or emery board. Put a small drop of Super Glue on the roughened end of the leader and carefully insert into the hollowed out end of the fly line. Finish by applying another drop of Super Glue over the bonded area. Allow to dry completely before using. This method produces a small, smooth, strong and durable attachment that will not hang up in the rod guides.

CURE FOR CURLY LEADERS

Using one of those rubber leader straighteners works, but they use heat to make the mono lose its memory. In my opinion, this tends to weaken the mono. I've used the following method for many years without a problem, and have, incidentally, reduced by one the number of items carried in my vest.

Grasp a section of leader about 2 1/2 feet long in both hands, starting with the butt end. Stretch it tightly between your hands and while taut, reach up with the ring finger of either hand and snap the leader once or twice. That should remove any coils from that section. If it hasn't, then you haven't pulled the section taut enough. Move down the leader a section at a time, slightly overlapping each section, until the leader is straight. Be sure to adjust the tension that you apply as you move toward the tippet—obviously the butt requires more tension than the tippet.

Another excellent way to straighten out the coils is to catch a five pound trout.

RESCUING FLIES

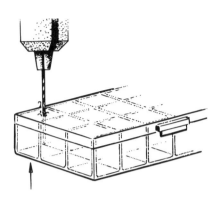

After all the effort required to tie up some nice flies we all hate to lose them unnecessarily. The greatest loss seems to result when wet, used flies are placed in fly boxes or books among unused, dry flies and you forget to remove the damp flies from the box for air drying at the end of the outing.

Eliminate this problem by taking an ordinary, see-through plastic fly box and drilling 9/16" holes, as many as possible, through the top and bottom of the box. The box is now properly ventilated. This container is then threaded on one end of the wader drawstring and knotted securely in place. When you're finished using a fly, snip it off and place it in this box. Now, it's a simple matter to dry and check over the flies you've fished when you get home.

SEND US YOUR TIPS

No individual fly tyer could possibly begin to conceive of the many fine ideas presented here, so we're dependent on the sharing of ideas within the fly-tying community. If you would like to share your tips with fellow fly tyers, please send them to us for possible use in future editions. They may be addressed to: Dick Stewart c/o Mountain Pond Publishing, PO Box 797, North Conway, NH 03860.

ADDITIONAL TIPS

ADDITIONAL TIPS

ADDITIONAL TIPS